Pearl Harbor

The Attack That Pushed The Us To Battle

(A Captivating Guide To The Surprise Military Strike By The Imperial Japanese Navy)

Michael Reif

Published By **Elena Holly**

Michael Reif

All Rights Reserved

Pearl Harbor: The Attack That Pushed The Us To Battle (A Captivating Guide To The Surprise Military Strike By The Imperial Japanese Navy)

ISBN 978-1-77485-671-0

No part of this guidebook shall be reproduced in any form without permission in writing from the publisher except in the case of brief quotations embodied in critical articles or reviews.

Legal & Disclaimer

The information contained in this ebook is not designed to replace or take the place of any form of medicine or professional medical advice. The information in this ebook has been provided for educational & entertainment purposes only.

The information contained in this book has been compiled from sources deemed reliable, and it is accurate to the best of the Author's knowledge; however, the Author cannot guarantee its accuracy and validity and cannot be held liable for any errors or omissions. Changes are periodically made to this book. You must consult your doctor or get professional medical advice before using any of the suggested remedies, techniques, or information in this book.

Upon using the information contained in this book, you agree to hold harmless the Author from and against any damages, costs, and expenses, including any legal fees potentially resulting from the application of any of the information provided by this guide. This disclaimer applies to any damages or injury caused by the use and application, whether directly or indirectly, of any advice or information presented, whether for breach of contract, tort, negligence, personal injury, criminal intent, or under any other cause of action.

You agree to accept all risks of using the information presented inside this book. You need to consult a professional medical practitioner in order to ensure you are both able and healthy enough to participate in this program.

Table Of Contents

Chapter 1: Sunday 7 December 1941, In The Morning. _____ 1

Chapter 2: The Unleashing Of An Empire 46

Chapter 3: Smaller Vessels Take Over The Lead _____ 69

Chapter 4: West Virginia Battles Fire And Flood _____ 80

Chapter 5: The Californian's Failure To Complete Its Mission _____ 89

Chapter 6: Maryland's Fortunate Escape _____ 102

Chapter 7: Other Heroes From The Time _____ 112

Chapter 8: Nagumo Decides _____ 132

Chapter 9: Effects _____ 143

Chapter 10: What Happened To Take Place On The Day Of Pearl Harbor? _____ 150

Chapter 1: Sunday 7 December 1941, In The Morning.

The Sunday of Pearl Harbor was a day of relaxation, rest and going to church. For the men who had just returned from their sea-based exercises there was a shore leave. A lot of them were not on their vessels on that tragic day. Some were still waking up slowly following an enjoyable night in Honolulu. There were the need to write letters as well as uniforms to be printed lockers to clean. However according to Marine Private Art Wells recalled, 'many died with a shoe still in their hands, thinking about the best way to compose the next paragraph in a letter or with their mouths wide when they started the next story from the sea'.

At the time of the attack, the majority of the early morning people were getting ready for church - one of the first victims were those on church boats who were being transported to the dockside. Other people had jobs to complete on Sundays or even without. When the first planes began to roar through Ford

Island, baker Dale Augerson was putting an apple pie batch in the oven of the West Virginia. The chocolate cakes, which were cooked were cooling as the PA announced the 'Fire and Rescue' Report on Ford Island.' On the Nevada the band was waiting to scream The Star Spangled Banner. The first notes were heard as the plane flew low enough to hit the deck. None of the marines was harmed, but just a moment afterward, they were left beneath a torn American flag, which was hanging at half-mast.

Lewis Shaw, a Pharmacist's Mate on the minelayer Oglala was in the shower. Also, on the warship Utah Robert Swift was busy making christmas cards to his loved ones in Tennessee. In a more mundane way, the attack that surprised men gave them without a choice about the clothes they'd fight in. Some were dressed in pyjamas and others in slippers. Mickey Ganitch on the Pennsylvania went to the general quarters wearing his football uniform.

Within 90 minutes, 2403 American servicemen died amid the wreckage, or floating in the harbor. Of the 301 aircrafts that were on the island that day, only 52 could be used. In the harbor, eight massive battleships were buried in the flaming waters. Airstrips, hangers docks, and planes, flames soared out into the sky. The atmosphere was filled with acrid smoke and the ocean was lit with fuel oil leaking from ruptured tanks of fuel. Pearl Harbor and Oahu's airstrips had been hit by one of the most powerful and most destructive surprise attacks in history. They had also said that it was unlikely to occur. Oahu was officially "The most powerful Fortress on Earth'.

America was asleep when it entered Pearl Harbor.

2. A rising empire

The end of the First World War the principal central powers (Germany Austria-Hungary, Germany and Turkey) were wiped out of their empires, while the allies who had won were tired and worn out. An international resentment towards conflict erupted as countries were attempting to limit their armaments. When she left the First World War America had tried to distance herself from global matters. President Wilson had, following his efforts to advance talks on the Versailles Treaty negotiations, returned home to discover that the Senate did not approve of the treaty until 1919. The same year, America chose not to join the newly-formed League of Nations. A few years later, America was a key participant at the Washington Naval Conference of 1921-22. By using her espionage skills, America defeated Japan in negotiating an agreement that severely thwarted Japan's imperial goals. In the agreement, American, British and Japanese navy was to be restricted to fleets of 5:5:3. Japan was a bit irritated by this reduction and began to view America as an enemy to its territorial goals. America's attempt to detach itself from international issues while causing annoyance to Japan was an extremely dangerous mix.

Tensions are rising in the Pacific

The enemy of America was not planning to retreat within herself. Japan began its expansion post-First World War by occupying Manchuria around 1931. The international reaction resulted in her deportation from in the League of Nations, but she did not let that deter the ambitions of Japan. In 1937, Japan began to invade China. The international community reacted with protests, which included a harsh criticism from America. It wasn't until Japan entered French Indochina in 1940 that America began to realize that her interests were at risk to the point that the need for action was urgent. President Roosevelt immediately stopped the export into Japan of any product that could be considered to be of military value. In the early part of 1941, it was obvious for America the fact that Japan was determined to invade and occupying the Philippines as well as also the Dutch East Indies. In response to this, Roosevelt was able to order the expansion of American troops on the Philippines. On the 25th of July 1941 America took the radical decision of blocking the entire amount of Japanese property inside the United States. In response, Japan advised Washington that the 'empire to safeguard its life, has to take action to safeguard the precious substances from the South Seas'. A week later, President Roosevelt made the final step to avoid war by imposing an embargo on exports of oil to Japan. He was hoping that Japan will now retreat from her enslavement. However, so huge was Japan's demand for oil it determinedly sought to capture the oil in this region of the Dutch East Indies at any cost. There was only one obstacle in her way and that was the American Pacific Fleet.

Yamamoto is convinced of the impossible

The person who influenced the decision to strike Pearl Harbor was Admiral Isoroku Yamamoto, the commander in chief of the Japanese Combined Fleet. When he was young, Yamamoto was present at the Battle of Tsushima in 1905 during which the Japanese navy had beaten an Russian fleet. It was the very first massive battle between warships made of steel. Japan did quite well. Following during the First World War Yamamoto's expertise in the field of aircrafts and carriers quickly was developed, giving Yamamoto the confidence to use the machines at a massive magnitude for the first time ever in the history of. Pearl Harbor, on the island of Oahu in the Hawaii islands, was going to be his test-bed for his concept of mass attacks.

In one way, Yamamoto's strategy was a bit out of line with military logic, as the plan was to target the enemy from the strongest point. However, Yamamoto asserted that his nation was forced to choose. Without American petroleum, Japan had either to concede defeat in her territorial expansion or acquire the oil from somewhere else. It would certainly result in conflict against America. United States - a war Japan cannot ever hope to be victorious in. If, however it was her first attempt to destroy the American Pacific Fleet. It was a gambler's decision driven by the issues of over-reach which were afflicting Japan in the latter half of 1940. With a single stroke, she would be able to take control of the Pacific and then be able to settle in the rich areas within the Pacific rim. To add to that, said Yamamoto that the loss of the US Pacific Fleet would so disillusion Americans Americans to the point that they'd be willing to participate in Japan's conquers.

Yamamoto begins to make plans

Yamamoto started his initial serious plan in February 1941. The plan was bold by any standards, and the problems were enormous. Oahu stood out with air bases in order to defend both the island as well as it's Pacific Fleet. Yamamoto will have plenty of targets. If Oahu receive warnings about his attack on the island, it will have plenty of troops to defend it.

However, it was the form of the harbour as well as its mooring styles that presented the most difficult obstacles for air attacks. The harbour was not able to provide air-based run-ins that were clear for planes, regardless of their angle. The mooring arrangements for the ships also presented problematic because the battleships were in pairs. Yamamoto was faced with an issue that torpedoes would not penetrate the vessels of the pair. The most significant issue was the depth of the harbour - just 40 feet. It was well-known that air-launched torpedoes sank between 50 and 100 feet before reaching their running-in depth. In shallow water, they would sink themselves into the mud and remain there for a while.

Priorities and targets

Yamamoto's strategy was simple. A large number of planes would arrive at dawn with the intention of frightening the local defenses. The initial target would be the airfields of Ford Island, Wheeler Field, Hickam Field, and Kaneohe Bay. (There were smaller airfields that did not figure in the list of his targets.) With the American aircraft destroyed before they could even launch their missiles, the Japanese planes would shift their attention to the moored vessels. Pilots would receive specific instructions on how to select top targets. Bombs and torpedoes weren't to be thrown away on smaller vessels, but any vessel close to the channel entrance was to be submerged with the intention that it could block the harbour's exit. (One effect of Yamamoto disregarding the small vessels was that they destroyed much more planes than the larger vessels. However, since Japan suffered so little loss of planes in the event the loss was not an important aspect of the overall result.) Surprisingly, no plane was dedicated in the destruction fuel dumps, or the repair workshops - an oversight that could result in the loss of Japan the country a lot of money.

There were also other weaknesses that could be identified that could be found in this Japanese plan. For one, sinking ships into shallow waters would make them easily salvageable. The second reason for attack on ships during a weekend harbor meant that significant amount of men and officers were on the shore - the latter were more difficult for replacement than vessels as they required years of training. A third factor was that an attack that failed to capture carriers could depart America with the three the most dangerous Pacific naval assets including submarines, carriers and the men. Yamamoto knew of the weaknesses however he believed there was no other choice then to take on the enemy.

Technical issues

In order for the mission to begin, Yamamoto had to find the solution to two technical challenges. The first was an explosive that could be dropped in shallow waters. In addition, considering the battleships that were moored to the inside of pairs the bomb needed to be one that could be able to penetrate the deck of a battleship. The work began to find ways to solve these issues. He also needed pilots who could handle the harsh conditions they would face at Oahu.

Training for air crews

The air assaults on Oahu were planned under the direction of Ace pilot commander Mitsuo Fuchida, who was an experienced participant in during the Second Sino-Japanese War in the 1930s. In September, he began to prepare the pilots for the difficult and risky task. To ensure that the training was as real as is possible, Fuchida chose a location at Kagoshima Bay on the southwest part of Japan. Today, it is more famous for dolphins rather as well as instructors, this bay offered the perfect mix of a narrow entrance that leads to a huge space of water with the steeply rising hills that surrounded. The port that was nearby Kagoshima was a good illustration of the crowded regions around Pearl Harbor. The port was occupied in the month of October 1941. Fuchida required the pilots to fly 160 knots at an altitude of just 165 feet, before descending lower to just 130 feet in order to launch their bombs. Their flight must be smooth and steady. For dive bomber pilots, they had to master the art of descending to let off their bombs at 1500 feet - considerably less than the safe maximum distance of 2500 feet. The pilots initially balked at these difficulties, but they soon were producing precise runs and a high proportion of hitting. Fastly Fuchida got his crew ready to prepare for Pearl Harbor.

The Yamamoto's First Air Fleet

In preparation for the attack Yamamoto brought together 6 aircraft carriers, 2 battleships two cruisers with heavy weights, one light cruiser, as well as sundry destroyers, submarines , and tankers. Five of them were midget submarines which were transported on mother submarines , before being released near to the entrance of Pearl Harbor. The ships were designed to transport more than 400 planes, of which 350 were to be involved in the battle. (The other planes comprised reserves and patrol planes that were used to defend those on the ships.)

The two waves attack

The size of the air fleet that Yamamoto had assembled , it was impossible to launch all of the aircraft at the same time, so Fuchida had planned a two-wave launch. This was a compromise as the second wave was going to attack without the added benefit of the surprise.

The First Air Fleet was to sail to sea under the direction by Vice Admiral Chuichi Nagumo, despite the fact Nagumo opposed his opposition to the Pearl Harbor venture.

Nagumo divided his forces into three carriers commands:

1. Nagumo: Carriers Akagi Kaga and Kaga.

2. Rear Admiral Tamon Yamaguchi: carriers Soryu and Hiryu.

3. Rear Admiral Chuichi Hara is a carrier of Shokaku along with Zuikaku.

The capacity of the carriers varied between the Hiryu with 54 planes aboard as well as the Akagi which had 72 planes. The planes they comprised B5N2 torpedo bombers D3A1 dive bombers as well as A6M2 fighters. These were the famous "Zeros" that were swift, maneuverable, and capable of beating any weapon the Americans could throw into the air.

Opposition

The fact that this Pearl Harbor venture ever got to this point was due to Yamamoto's steadfast determination. He was challenged by many colleagues, including the Captain Sadatoshi Tomioka, who was the Chief of Naval Operations on the General Staff. In addition to generally opposing the offensive, Tomioka also tried to restrict Yamamoto's forces to just three instead of six. It was only when it became apparent that Yamamoto was going to quit in the event of not being provided with 6 carriers, did Tomioka reluctantly agree to.

The day that is fatal is picked

Around 11 October that the date was finally decided to launch the assault: 7 Dec 1941 (Hawaii time). The weekday was vital. For example, the Pacific Fleet was almost never in action on a Sunday and there no alerts for practice on Sundays. An early attack could reveal an unoccupied fleet, and empty airfields.

3. An island with arms, but an unprepared

The Army and its bases

On paper Yamamoto was facing the formidable enemy. On the island Oahu was in essence a huge fortress. However, the army's presence wasn't there to defend the city of Honolulu but to guard that of the Pacific Fleet when it was in arbor as well as the bases of the military while it was at sea. Major General Walter Short, the commanding general had 43,000 troops (including those from the Air Corps) at his at his disposal. Short was supported in his duties by Major General Henry Burgin of the coastal artillery, and Major General Frederick Martin, who commanded the Hawaiian Air Force. In addition, there were two infantry divisions in Schofield Barracks.

Short was confident that his troops were equipped to defend his fleet and bases. The same confidence was echoed with the Army Chief of Staff in Washington and told the president Roosevelt on April 11, 1941, that Oahu was the'strongest Fortress anywhere in the world'. But, Short had an unfortunate perception of his priorities. The greatest threat to the island stemmed through acts of sabotage committed by the large Japanese population. Although he acknowledged possible attack but he considered it to be a distant possibility considering how simple it would be to deter an invader. However, he never for a second thought the possibility of an attack via air. Oahu was located nearly 4000 miles away from Japan and it was likely that any attacking force would be stopped from Pacific Fleet. Pacific Fleet.

The primary method for island defence was the air bases of the army located at Wheeler Field, Hickam Field and Bellows Field. Wheeler Field, more or more or less situated in the center in the islands, served as the primary airbase of the army, and housed chase planes in when the attacks took place. The base itself was massive and had an enormous mess hall that could hold 2000 people. Hickam Field was located on the east end of the channel, which linked Pearl Harbor to the sea. It was constructed over 2000 acres of coral covered in soil reef, it was operating since 1937. On the 1st of November, 1940, it had been converted into the 18th Bombardment Wing (Heavy). The day of the attack there were B-17s in the number of 12 33 B-18s, along with thirteen A-20 Douglas Havocs in the air. The final air base for the army was located at Bellows Field on the south-east coast. It was the home of surveillance as well as pursuit teams. It was a tiny facility with just 21 planes in the air at the time of the assault. (The principal bases for the military, Schofield barracks, lay close the Wheeler Field. It was not a significant factor in the events that transpired that day.)

The navy was at Oahu

The prize Yamamoto sought was American Pacific Fleet - or the most of it possible. On the 7th of December, there was around 90-100 American vessels (no two sources can agree on the exact amount) in the harbor. No matter the numbers the vessels that were of the greatest fascination in the eyes of Japanese were the Japanese are the 3 carriers (Enterprise, Lexington, and Saratoga) as well as eight battleships as well as eight cruisers, and 30 destroyers. However, the carriers were prominently not present on the morning of the assault.

Alongside the air bases for the army The fleet also had three air bases with its own. The principal navy airport - Ford Island - sat in the middle of the harbour. It was the home of

Patrol Wing 2, where squadrons 22and 23 were located. 24. On the 7th of December, there were 81 planes on the base, and 72 were on the ground or in readiness for flight with 4 hours ' notice. It was among the bases with the highest activity in the area that day as it had seven aircraft on patrol and four more ready to fly at 10 minutes' notice.

It was the navy's Patrol Wing 1 was based at Kaneohe Bay. This airstrip was situated on a peninsular that extended out into the ocean on the east of the isle. It was a perfect landing strip but vulnerable to sea-based attacks. The base was under construction in 1941 , and contained the three squadrons of air police. On the 7th of December at dawn, the 33 PBY Catalinas belonging to patrol squadrons 11 12, 13 and 14 were mainly set up on the ground, while other were bobbing gently across the water.

The third base of naval air force included that of the Ewa Marine Air Corps Station that was located west of the entrance to the arbor. There were around 50 planes based there with

11 F4F-3 fighters as well as 26 SBD-1s and 2s diving bomber/scout aircrafts.

Radar Oahu's cutting-edge technology

In theory , the island's defense would have been assured with the help of radars, but America's radar expertise was abysmal in 1941. According to an official history of the army of the time, six mobile radar stations in the islands. But, as the historian , '[they] hadn't ever been integrated with an operational aircraft warning system'. This is a courteous way of saying that the military in general , and Short specifically did not appreciate the installation nor did they appreciate their importance. In the way it was used by the radar, it was ineffective against an attack of surprise since it was only operational during the day for four hours and some units had no direct contact with the command center. There was no phone in any of the units. It was arithmetic, however, which revealed the error in Short's reasoning. The radar could spot planes that were up to 150 miles from the plane. It gave approximately a one hour warning of planes that were approaching. The planes must be detected well before they could reach Oahu. Also, Short had about 30 minutes from receiving a radar signal to get his planes into the air to be successful in preventing an attack. However, there was no place was there Oahu was there a command center capable of making and implementing a decision within such a period.

4. Oahu's four defenders

Since when Pearl Harbor, the day of Pearl Harbor disaster, politicians as well as commissions, committees and even pundits have debated and debated the attack. It is a constant discussion that always goes all the way back to four main men on Oahu on that day. (And as we'll examine, their relationship to Washington.)

Admiral Husband Kimmel

The Commander-in-Chief of US Pacific Fleet Admiral Husband Kimmel, took up his position in February 1941. After a while, Kimmel informed his Chief of Naval Operations that he thought that a surprise attack against Pearl Harbor was possible and that measures were being made to prevent the possibility of such an attack. It's unclear what Kimmel did, but in any event the primary duty of protecting the ship and the island was the responsibility of the army. The army owned the radar stations as well as base airfields where the bulk of the bombers and fighters were able to take off. The man was described as hardworking. Kimmel has also been accused of giving too much importance to details and not assigning enough responsibility. Kimmel would re-evaluate the small choices he'd previously made, and ponder things he should be able to delegate to others. While his attention ought to have been focused on the larger picture at Oahu however, his thoughts were often elsewhere. His Oahu post led to his dismissal and early retirement.

Lieutenant General Walter Short

The person responsible for the security of the island and responsible for securing the fleet at sea was the commander of the Hawaiian

Department of the American Army Major General Walter Short. Similar to Kimmel and Kimmel, he also made his debut in February. He was able to climb quickly to the position when he received his appointment in 1902. In his time in the First World War he had been the assistant chief of staff for the Third Army. Before being promoted to Oahu on February 11, 1941,, he was a corps commander. A dull plodder with no inclination to be a leader who was proactive and leadership, he did not even have an action plan for any attempt to invade the island. Short was to meet similar fate to Kimmel by being demotioned and forced retirement.

Rear Admiral Patrick Bellinger

Another important person in Hawaii is Rear Admiral Patrick Bellinger. As the commander of Patrol Wing Two he was the naval air chief on December 7. His chief of staff Lieutenant Commander Ramsay who gave out the famous message , 'AIR RAID, PEARLHARBOR, This is NOT a drill'. Bellinger's fame lasted through Pearl Harbor and he later was named Commander Air

Force, Atlantic Fleet. Bellinger's success in the post resulted in him receiving the Distinguished Service Medal and he was praised as a skilled and effective administrator and for his 'powerful leadership', and for his 'efficiency level of readiness to fight' Bellinger developed - the latter quality being a glaring omission from Kimmel Short and Kimmel. Short.

Major General Frederick Martin

The final key person is Major General Frederick Martin, who was in charge of the Hawaiian Air Force. An knowledgeable airman - Martin had been involved with aircrafts from his time in the First World War - his reputation would last for a long time despite the huge losses his forces suffered. At Oahu Martin was too enthused to accept Short's opinion in which sabotage was the biggest threat to the bases, and - possibly against his best judgment - put his planes in a mass exactly as Short did. However, Martin was in a very poor state of health and shouldn't be in his position on the 7th of December. Martin suffered from a chronic stomach ulcer. It was so bad that he was sent to the hospital just around an hour after the attack began.

5. Not enough warnings

Yoshikawa's island tours

The possibility of a Japanese strike at Pearl Harbor would involve transporting hundreds of planes and carriers across 4000 miles of ocean. What if the Pacific Fleet weren't at the harbor when planes arrived? This is a non-sensical scenario, and could only be prevented by vigilant surveillance. Fortunately , Yamamoto Hawaii was home to a significant Japanese population, so anyone who saw Japanese looking around were not likely to be at them as if they were out of place. Furthermore that it was not illegal to view the docks, harbours and airfields as long as you did not intrude into the areas. This was the beginning of the arduous but public activities in the name of Takeo Yoshikawa. Yoshikawa had been an Intelligence Officer who completed his studies at the

Japanese Naval Academy in 1933 at the highest rank in his class. After arriving in Hawaii in the middle of March, 1941, He rented a home which overlooked Pearl Harbor and set about exploring the island, navigating the island in taxis, and traveling in the glass-bottomed vessel to aid in estimating harbour depths. The numerous reports, encoded with the unique Purple code, were returned to Japan via an local Japanese consulate. Yoshikawa continued to work until December 4, when the message "east wind, rain' in a forecast for weather warned Yoshikawa to burn and shred any evidence of his work. Yoshikawa's work was sometimes complemented by others' work such as two naval officers who took a flight to Japan in October, to spend a week on the island collecting data about harbour depths operations, fleet activities, and the construction of hangers. They even rented an aircraft for private use and snapped pictures of the airfields and the harbour. However, it was Yoshikawa's actions that proved the evidence of which Yamamoto was able to construct his attack. Yoshikawa was the one who informed Japan what ships were in port and where they were berthed. The reports he provided verified the regularity of Pacific Fleet activities out on Mondays or Tuesday, returning on Sunday or Saturday. He also confirmed that the fleet traveled 45 miles during its exercise.

"The most powerful Fortress on Earth'

The opinions on the vulnerability of Oahu as well as Pearl Harbor were varied widely in 1941 and 1940. The person with most influence over the matter is General George Marshall, the Army Chief of Staff in Washington. General Marshall referred to Oahu the'strongest defense fortress on earth', in an account which was presented to the President Roosevelt during April of 1941. However, Marshall could only envisage an adversary who wanted to conquer Oahu and, therefore, he highlighted its massive garrison and its 3000 Anti-Aircraft (AA) gun. Concerning the notion of an attack led by a carrier, he stated that these vessels could be attacked by air within a range of 775 miles. The closer they got to the target, the more devastating the attack could be. This argument may be valid except for one fact Marshall decided to ignore: Oahu did not have enough aircraft to conduct sufficient patrols. As Yamamoto demonstrated that it was easy to sneak into the late at night and make it to close to 200 miles from the island and not be detected by any submarine or plane. Once carriers got that close it would be late for the planes of Oahu to begin a swift response. The only risk Marshall saw was the possibility of the possibility of sabotage. To avoid this, he advocated increasing the military's control over people living in the area. A surprise air strike was impossible and unlikely.

The locals were more realistic of the dangers facing the island. Martin and Bellinger were apprehensive in a report they wrote to be submitted to Rear Admiral Claude Bloch, Commander of the Fourteenth Naval District. Their three main conclusions should be a shivering read to anyone who read them again on the 8th of December. Martin as well as Bellinger believed that Japan would launch an attack prior to declaring war and that it was a carrier-based strike and would take place in the early hours of dawn. A reason that they cited was that the island didn't have enough patrol planes to spot the approaching intruder. They suggested - even though they knew they didn't have planes capable of doing the job - that there be daytime security patrols all throughout the entire island.

The cry of the real war

In the midst of discussions on the dangers in Oahu, Henry Stimson (Secretary of War) and Frank Knox (Secretary of the Navy) were contemplating the bigger wars within Europe as well as North Africa. While America was not a belligerent nation however, she provided significant assistance to Britain by protecting the western region of the Atlantic. Both secretaries agreed with the President to build the Atlantic Fleet at the expense of the Pacific. The real conflict in Europe represented a greater threat to the global order than the hypothetical war within the Pacific. In the wake of this decision, Kimmel had to surrender the carrier Yorktown along with four destroyers in the latter part of April. This decision could have caused Kimmel as well as Short to minimize the possibility of the possibility of a Japanese attack. If Washington believed it was safe to send ships across the Atlantic Did they really have to be concerned about Japan?

Farthing's appeal to massed B-17s

In August 1941, it came to Colonel William Farthing, commander of Hickam Field, to raise concerns regarding the security of Oahu. The reasoning behind the report he prepared upon the instruction by the War Department was irrefutable: Oahu's security was contingent on preventing enemies' carriers from getting close enough for them to fly their aircrafts. One way to accomplish this was by conducting 360-degree patrols throughout the day. He pleaded with Washington to provide 180 B-17s. He declared, was a'small amount of troops compared to the importance that this post had'. A few months later, Secretary of War Stimson sent all of his remaining B-17s over to Oahu which included twelve machines. They landed just as Japanese were advancing.

Japan's diplomatic smokescreen

When Yamamoto had been planning an attack While Yamamoto was planning his strike, the Japanese government was seeking peace. They wanted something straightforward, but bizarre that they could occupy French Indochina, the Dutch East Indies and Malaya without American interference. To achieve this, Tokyo dispatched the Ambassador Kichisaburo Nomura Washington at the close the month of November in 1940. Nomura was a mariner who graduated from the Japanese Naval Academy in 1898. In 1916-18, he served as the naval attache of the United States and he also took part in the Washington Naval Conference. By the year 1941, he had been discharged from the navy, attaining an admiral's rank. It's not clear if the admiral realized that he had been selected mainly for his inexperience as for knowledge of the navy However, it was not long before he realised that he was going to serve as the conduit of useless concessions that had a sole aim that was to keep Americans in the room at the conference table. At the end of 1941, when Yamamoto was frantically planning his assault force as well as preparing his attack force, the unlucky Nomura was often summoned to meet the Secretary of State Hull to discuss the most current Japanese ideas. However, the closer Japan reached the 7th of December the more these plans turned out to be a cover-up for their malicious intentions.

Similar to how the Japanese were watching the Americans on Oahu as well, the Americans were keeping an eye for the Japanese. Every communication between Japan and its Embassy at Washington as well as its consulate at Honolulu were routinely read. The particular code, known as "Purple," was discovered in the summer of 1940. The decryptions were referred to as 'Magic', and were as valuable to Americans just as Ultra secret codes were for the British. However, the code breakers were more eager to break codes than to reveal the results. In September 1941, when it was discovered that the Japanese consulate at Honolulu received the request of Tokyo to make a grid that included Pearl Harbor with the location of every vessel, Washington failed to pass the information the information to Kimmel as well as Short, who was in Hawaii. Why would the Japanese want to know the precise location of the ships , other than to prepare for an attack by air? Who would be the first to be aware that an air attack was in the works? However, neither Kimmel or Short was ever informed of the request. In the meantime, Yoshikawa provided the grid, assigning codes like "KS" to indicate the repair dock, and "KT" to refer to the Navy dock. In the meantime, Yoshikawa began to show an additional attention to Wheeler Field and Hickam.

No action is required

In the days prior to the attack America was not devoid of warnings about what was to follow. The Ambassador Joseph Grew in Tokyo was among the first to alert the world. (Having previously served as an assistant to the Ambassador to Germany at the start of the First World War Grew perhaps was more sensitive to the signals.) There was an election of the government in Tokyo on the 17th of October. The new premier was general Hideki Tojo. Grew quickly realized that Tojo was an individual who was willing to risk war instead of turning his back on Japan's imperial goals. On the 3rd of November Grew warned Washington that Japan could make an attack at any time, and in a 'dramatic , and dangerous' way.

A couple of weeks afterward - right as Yamamoto's ships were being assembled - Admiral Harold Stark, Chief of Naval Operations, warned Kimmel of a possible surprise strike at Guam or in the Philippines. While Stark was not explicit about Hawaii, Kimmel should surely have known that conflict in the Pacific could have grave consequences to the Pacific Fleet and its base.

The next day, a message in the name of General Marshall was sent to General Short and Admiral Kimmel. It warned them of an attack from the enemy 'at any time and advised them to conduct'such surveillance and other actions as you think appropriate'. The men did not take any decision.

The Navy Department sent Kimmel a more specific warning at that time. The dispatch was intended to be taken as a warning to war and to anticipate an aggressive action by Japan within a couple of days. Short was also warned issued by his War Department. The two men did not take any action. Most importantly there was no effort to increase air patrols. (After an attack Kimmel claimed that he didn't even know what the word 'war warning was.)

The only move Short did in the final few weeks was to assemble all his planes in the form of a square, so that they could be safer from saboteur attacks. It took several hours to separate the planes and then get them in the air. In addition, the tight packing made sure that if one plane ignited, rest would soon follow. Strangely Short himself had highlighted the danger in a letter addressed to the Adjutant General back in March. He recommended a greater dispersal among the aircrafts.

Another sign that something was going on was the night between the 30th of November and the 1st of December The night before, Japan suddenly changed all of its navy service callsigns. The usual practice was to change the call frequency every two years. This had happened twice in the course of a month, and immediately there was a decrease in signal traffic. In Washington it was believed as a sign it was the case that Japanese fleet was in the sea and with a purposeful mind.

The next day, on the 3rd of December Kimmel received the information that Washington was to consider to be one of two crucial warnings that he issued (the one that was the 'war ' message). Kimmel was informed that Japanese embassies across the globe were ordered to destroy the codes, ciphers and encryption and to destroy all documents that were classified. Nobody could have interpreted this to mean something other than the impending onset of war. None other than Kimmel would have believed that, which is. Kimmel did not see anything of importance in this message , and then filed it away.

6. A rampant empire

To sea and in war

It was on 1 November, that The Japanese Imperial Council finally decided to declare war against America. The 5th of November Yamamoto received the formal instruction of the Navy General Staff to prepare for war with the United Sates, Britain and the Netherlands. The date of the war was set for the beginning of December. There were five risky weeks during which military preparations were completed at home, while in Washington Nomura was required to keep the illusion that Japan was seeking a peaceful resolution to her talks. Over the next few weeks, there was nothing changes in the instructions which Nomura got from his counterpart at the Japanese Foreign Office. His task was to delay for a period of time. However, Tokyo did not intend on telling the misguided and unintentionally well-intentioned Nomura the entire story. Instead, his bosses simply asked Nomura to settle the Japanese-American relationship on the 25th of November'. There was a strict deadline of the 29th of November, as he was told. If he didn't agree by that date it was inevitable that things would take place'. What "things" wasn't told.

In the final week of November, Nagumo's vessels began to congregate in Hittokapu Bay in the Kurile Islands. The remoteness of the area virtually ensured that nobody would be able to see the vast collection of vessels. Then, on the 26th of November The First Air Fleet weighed anchor and set sail toward Oahu. The route was carefully selected to reduce the chance of coming across American vessels. A single merchant vessel or warship in exercise or a single patrol plane could be enough to trigger American suspicions. To stay clear of such confrontations, the fleet would follow the northern route, traveling towards the east for a period of about 3 December. At that point, it would be about close to the north shore of Oahu and then would change direction to the south in order to confront the adversaries.

The weather conditions on the northern route contributed to Nagumo's woes. There was an abrasive sea. and the wind intense and sometimes the large ships sank to as high as 45 degrees. Deck work was dangerous and many people were swept away into the ocean. There were no stops in search and rescue. It could sabotage the timetable and put the fleet at risk of being observed. At least, the decreased visibility from the fog and fog was at Nagumo's back.

While the huge ships plowed the rough oceans, the reports continued coming in from Honolulu with information about the vessels at Pearl Harbor. It was also reassuring report that there were not American vessels at Lahaina - the anchorage off the west coast of Oahu which the fleet often employed. However, there was no sign of American carriers. This was extremely disappointing for Nagumo. Nagumo was not only unable to engage them, but they could appear in his radar at any time. (None one of the Nagumo's vessels was equipped with radar.)

Within a couple of days of beginning the voyage, Nagumo's ships needed to refill their tanks - an extremely risky task that was not previously attempted under such challenging situations. To refill the ships, they initially slowed down, then carried a tanker on tow. The fuel line was connected across the vessel. The umbilically connected ships raced through until the task was finished. However, it was Nagumo's unfortunate luck that his captains faced terrible weather conditions that were extremely challenging on the trip. Sometimes towing lines failed sometimes, and the weather halted work, and in some instances the refuelling process was stopped when sunset came over the operations.

On the 2nd of December, Nagumo received an encouraging message from Admiral Ugaki his Chief of Staff in Tokyo The attack was in progress. (Up until that point, successful diplomatic efforts could have resulted in the mission being delayed.) Nagumo displayed to his ships"Climb the Mount Niitaka 1208'. The reference to the highest peak in Japan and the 8th of November (7 Dec. Hawaiian time) revealed everything. Everything seemed to be going according exactly as planned. But, unbeknownst to Nagumo the 5th of December brought about the beginning of an event that would be a major blow to the aftereffects of Nagumo's assault. The carrier Lexington had left Pearl Harbor. The following day, the carrier Enterprise fighting an incoming storm, abandoned her plan for a return trip in Pearl Harbor that day. Three of the US Pacific Fleet carriers were at sea and were unable to get away from the destruction to follow.

Preparing to attack

As Nagumo approached Oahu the entire focus of his mind was focused on the possibility of being observed. As of the 6th December, there were still no signs of ships or planes. With only 600 miles to Nagumo's goal, it appeared Nagumo was successful in defeating the Oahu defenses.

As of now, Yoshikawa despatched his last harbour report, stating that there was not a sign of any air reconnaissances at Pearl Harbor. The stage was set for a surprise attack without opposition. If the Americans hadn't already made things easier for the Japanese Lieutenant

Colonel Hoppaugh of the Hawaiian Air Force requested that the local radio station KGMB stay on air through the night to aid in the guiding of the B-17s that were expected to arrive. These would not have been the sole planes that could utilize that signal for homing. Another example of the oahu's complacency was when General Short returned home with his wife following an evening of entertainment. While looking out over the sparkling harbour, he looked at his wife and asked her 'What a potential target an ideal target!' At the time that General Short made the comment, there were 23 Japanese submarines positioned off shores of Oahu ready to strike any American ships moving through or out. A noose had already been put around his neck.

Deadline for the deadly

The day that ended the attack, Japan executed her last dangerous act of treachery in her shady "negotiations" in her counterparts in the United States. They planned to mail a lengthy diplomatic note from her Washington Embassy for presentation to the State Department at exactly 1.00 midnight local time. The note was intended to break the diplomatic relationship and declared war. The first part of the note was scheduled arriving at the Embassy around 8.00 am on December 6 at a time when Nagumo was only 600 miles away from his goal.

Of course it was the Americans were also receiving the message simultaneously at the Naval Department's Security Section. At 7.00 pm, the thirteen pieces that were received had been transliterated and decoded. The translated text was then rushed through Washington and reached the President in the late evening. However, part 14 was not there.

In the Japanese Embassy, Nomura was waiting for the fourteenth piece. However, when it did arrive the staff was slow in decoding the message while the translator was not perfect - the entire thing needed to be rewritten before Nomura could properly hand it over for Secretary Hull. Thus, when Nomura was finally able to deliver the letter to Hull at 2:20pm on the 7th of December Pearl Harbor was already a burning debris. The note ended with "The

Japanese Government is sorry to have to inform to the American Government that because of the policy to be taken by the American Government, they cannot but think it's impossible to come to an agreement in further negotiations. After having read the note, Hull was able to look at Nomura and asked:

"In my fifty years of service to the public, I've never come across an official document filled with the most notorious falsehoods or disinformation ... at an amount so massive that I had no idea until now that any government anywhere on earth was capable of speaking the lies.'

It was not the content of the note that concerned Hull and his fellow colleagues - in the end, it didn't actually declare an official declaration of war. The most alarming part was the cover instruction to Nomura that read: "Will the Ambassador be able to submit an email to the United States Government (if feasible in the event of a meeting with the Secretary of States) our response to the United States at 11:30 p.m. on 7th of the 7th, at your time. It was evident to Colonel Rufus Bratton General of Military Intelligence of The Far East, that something important and very urgent was to happen within the Pacific.

Chapter 2: The Unleashing Of An Empire

The final warning for Pearl Harbor

At around midnight on 6 December, the five mother submarines started the process of releasing their children from on the shores of Oahu. The final release was completed around 3.30 am, and the vessels left towards the entrance channel to the harbour.

The Type A Ko-hyoteki midget submarines were 46 tons in weight and could travel around 100 miles. The submarines had a two-man crew, one to control the vessel and the other to ensure the speed and trim. The submarines' driving was not an easy job. The crew was given almost no space to work, and the submarines were difficult to maneuver and trim. In this instance the submariners had to get into a harbour that thousands of of eyes looked over the water each day. And that, even when Oahu was at its lowest alert, patrol boats were guarding the entry point to the channel.

One of these vessels is the tiny 195 ton coastal minesweeper Condor was in the process of patrolling as Honolulu was sleeping. When Ensign McCloy looked into the dark and saw a peculiar white streak of water. He initially thought it was just a random wave, but the more you look at it, the more convinced he became looking at the periscope's wake. He called Quartermaster Uttrick. Uttrick looked at the wave. It was indeed an Periscope. It was 3.57 am Condor indicated by blinker light at the destroyer Ward "Sighted a submerged vessel in the west course at a speed of nine knots.' Ward set off to locate the intruder. The officers of Condor as well as those of Ward were aware of how significant what they observed: Pearl Harbor was under attack.

A few hours later, Condor and another minesweeper called the Crossbill were taken off their patrol. The anti-submarine net that guards the entry channel opened as they approached, and both ships eased through the harbor. The net did not shut again until hours later. This was enough space for midget submarines to go unnoticed into the harbor.

Then Capt. William Outerbridge of the Ward was searching in vain for the submarine mentioned by Condor. At 5.36 am, he realized the search was at the wrong way due to his misinterpretation the signal of Condor. Outerbridge changed his pattern of search. After an hour, Outerbridge's Ward received a call from the cargo vessel Antares of an unidentified object in the starboard side of her. He contacted the navy air patrol, and within minutes , two smoke flares had indicated the area in which the object was seen. In no time, Ward's deck officer had the object on his radar. He called Outerbridge who raced towards the bridge only to be rewarded with seeing a tower of conning rising out from the water.

Outerbridge was ordered to go to go full speed ahead. Ward went from a formal 5 knots to an accelerating 25 as she took towards the submarine. At first, it appeared like she was preparing to hit the enemy but she was able to pass at 560 yards. When Ward was within reach, her three and one guns went into flames. The bullet from the first gun sailed harmlessly over the submarine , but the shot from the second struck the vessel directly on the waterline. The midget submarine was sunk. The damaged vessel floundered in the sea as she was hit by the Ward dropped four deep charges in her. The Seaman Russell Reetz felt the Ward topple and shake as 450kg of TNT sank up, and he worried that the ship could sink also. When the doomed submarine began sinking within 1200 feet of the ocean there was a huge patch of oil appeared on level with the ocean top of the water - it was the only thing left to prove the existence of the vessel. Outerbridge confirmed the sinking to the harbour noting that 'we have fired shots at as well as dropped deep charges on submarines operating in the defense seas', however, no action was taken. Outerbridge did not know he fired one of the very first rounds fired during the Second World War. It was two days into his role as commander officer. (This was the beginning of a remarkable career in which he fought on Normandy as well as Cherbourg in France as well as in Ormoc, Mindoro, Lingayon Gulf, Okinawa and Japan in the Pacific.)

Zero hour

At 5.50 am, the First Air Fleet was 220 miles away from Oahu. This was the time for take on. Nagumo transformed his transporters towards the wind, and increased speed in order to provide his planes with the most lift they could get when they took off. Each time Fuchida took his planes up through the air to create an overhead. At 6.20 AM, Fuchida signaled signals for his devastating force to head for Pearl Harbor. His armada of death was around 90 minutes' flight from the unaware Pacific Fleet. Shimazaki's personal flight began around 7.15 am. All the practice on Kagoshima Bay was now to bring its benefits.

As Fuchida was getting closer to Oahu He spotted the useful signal of KGMB. After re-aligning the flight to follow its route He then signaled his pilots to follow suit. Five minutes later, Fuchida was able to clearly observe Oahu with his binoculars. The island was silent beneath the clear blue sky which there was no enemy plane visible. He grabbed his rocket rifle and let off a flash - an indication to his planes that a surprise was over.

The Radar issue

The shrewd use of radar was vital in securing Britain from being snatched by the Luftwaffe during the Battle of Britain in 1940 However, the radar stations guarding Oahu were not in a position to handle what struck the island the day before. The station that spotted the planes that came in was located in the northwestern part of Oahu and two soldiers, Joseph Lockard and George Elliot were working. Elliot was in training and Lockard did not have any prior experience that could be relevant to what he was going to witness. As their shift was coming to the end of their shift at 7.00 am, the truck which was supposed to take the group to breakfast hadn't been delivered. Instead of turning off their radar - it shut in when it was 7.00 morning during the week on Sundays - they played with the radar for a while. At 7.02 am Elliot noticed something that appeared amazing. It was like the tracks of a massive mass of planes that was 136 miles away. It would be impossible to do this on a Sunday, with only a few planes due in were a handful of B-17s from the continent.

Lockard was confused. He looked over his equipment. There was nothing wrong. After Elliot's advice and advice, he contacted to the Harbour Intercept Centre to report the sighting. He left a message for an officer in the army and then returned to his screen. As he got closer and closer, the apparent planes appeared. After 20 miles, the interference from nearby high ground deformed the image, and the two men lost sight on the aircrafts. At this point, Elliot and Lockard stopped the station and left the post. The moment Lockard's message reached the 1st Lieutenant Kermit Tyler at the Harbour Intercept Centre he assumed that the plots were B-17s he expected and did not take any further action. (Like Elliot, Tyler had not received any training for his position and was not well-versed to run the centre by himself.)

The first wave attacked

When Fuchida's initial wave attack planes crossed the shores of Oahu without being noticed and unopposed, he could see the harbour off in the distant distance. Fuchida's cries of 'Tora Tora, Tora' Tiger Tiger, Tiger, Tiger was broadcast back to the carrier. The code confirmed that Oahu was taken by shock.

The planes of his were to strike the battleships on three occasions:

1. The initial flight comprising 90 B5N bombers - some equipped with bombs and others equipped with torpedoes - was directed by Fuchida and was meant to take on the battleships. (Had the carriers not been there they could have attacked them too.)

2. The second mission, headed by Lieutenant-Commander Kakiuchi Takahashi was comprised of 54 Aichi D3A dive bombers. Their objectives comprised Wheeler Field and Ford Island.

3. The third aircraft was piloted by Lieutenant Shigeru Thisaya. It had 45 A6M Mitsubishi Zeros that were used for attacks on airfields.

The second group of 171 planes around one hour after, commanded by Squadron Commanding Officer Shigekazu Shimazaki. The planes would attack the same targets and to destroy any remaining aircrafts, ships and other facilities. Shimazaki was a formidablely accomplished pilot and instructor with battle experience from The Second Sino Japanese War. He did not only make it through 7 December, but continue to cause further damage to his allies until his death in combat in the early part of 1945.

8. Breakfast surprise at the airfields

When they looked up at the island, Japanese pilots could spot the empty airfields. Patrol planes and bombers were neatly in tightly packed groups. There was not even a person in sight. The mess buildings were the only ones to show little evidence of life as people looked for breakfast. The planes swiftly crashed into the silence of a sleepy island. At Wheeler they arrived out of the northern part. Kaneohe was attacked by the east. In Pearl Harbor planes came from all directions on the compass.

Fuchida using his bombers B5N flew into the battleships. Takahashi was heading towards Wheeler Field and Ford Island with his Aichi D3A dive bombers. And Itaya took in his Mitsubishi A6M Zero to attack various airfields. The bombs weighing 800kg would tear the decks off of battleships, while the 452 lb torpedoes will cut through the hulls of the strongest ship. the strafing rounds will rip apart fragile planes and vulnerable people in the ground.

Hickam Field

The airfield for the army at Hickam Field was the first area to be a victim of the Japanese attack. The first planes landed through the field around 7.55 am before they flew into the dockyard. Following them were four D3A1 dive bombers. Their bombs crashed into the airport's infrastructure. Mess halls, engineering buildings and hangers were destroyed. Instantly, flames and smoke came out of the building. Twenty-two pilots who were in the process of getting their bombers out to train were destroyed quickly. The dive bombers then were able to focus their attention on aircrafts that were on the ground. The A-20s, B-18s and the B-17s had been neatly parked from wingtip to the wingtip. The first blasts hit an unparked B-17 as well as B-18s that were nearby. The flames that resulted from these extended to other planes. In a matter of minutes, chaos reigned.

At first, Sergeant Harry Guilliams and his fellows stared at the intruders in stupefied disbelief. They'd had no experience in recognition of planes and mistakenly thought the planes for navy aircraft. When the bombs started to fall, Guilliams discovered his mistake and rushed to grab an assault rifle. He quickly struck the plane, which as he remembered,'made a circular impact and then struck a structure'.

Other soldiers who were on the base at that time were more gritty. Joseph Pesek, still in civilian clothing during the attack, put on a pair of overalls when he heard the sound of the gun. While he was running through the parade grounds, he came across Dave Jacobson and three other men struggling to put up the First

World War water-cooled machine gun. Pesek had some knowledge of the weapon , so he put the gun up for them and continued on his way. A few minutes later, the Japanese made a direct strike against Jacobson as well as his crew. Pesek said that the only way to identify Dave was by spotting an area of his finger that had his ring in its place.'

Some survived even at a high cost. Carl Drechsler remembered little of the incident. He heard the message to duty stations, and been back to the hanger. He was drinking and talking, aircrafts of the enemy roared into view. A person shouted "It's an Air attack" and Drechsler took cover to get away. He was shocked to discover that was that he was blind and caught on fire. He went to sleep and, when he woke up with his eyes restored after which he discovered a huge cut within his shoulder. The arm was subsequently saved by surgeons however, he was badly burned and it took ten months before he could return to work.

In the midst chaos and gunfire , the men of the 428th Signal Maintenance company were determined to repair the broken base communications system. They had two trucks each containing seven people, drove across the field, distributing telephone wires from a spool on the side. The men swung stakes into the ground , and connecting the wires.

As the strafing and bombing continued the frantic efforts were undertaken to get the handful of serviceable aircrafts in the air. Pesek was helping them with their arming up and returning to the hanger to pick up another shipment with 0.5 calibre ammo when he heard that there was nothing left. He turnedand walked out of the massive sliding doors, and a few seconds later, a bomb crashed through the roof of the hanger. The hanger appeared to rise in the air, however Pesek was knocked to the ground and was sprayed in white clay. As he lay on the ground, dazed one of the men threw a bottle whisky into his hand. He couldn't even hold it, as he was shaken with fear.

In this chaotic blaze came B-17s from the mainland. Major Truman Landon was leading the twelve aircrafts after their 14-hour flight across the ocean from mainland. The planes had dived and ducks to avoid Japanese planes they ran into. It was so secure that nearly everyone in the island knew the planes were due to arrive that morning. As a result, the island's AA took action against B-17s. Vic Bourasaw, Chief Petty Officer on the Ramsay explained how he observed one of the lumbering aircrafts enter the air with Japanese fighters at its rear and Oahu Aircraft AA shooting at it on the ground. The gunner and the tail gunner were simply sat there and taking in the sights, but not firing a shot of ammunition to return fire. The pilots skillfully avoided the AA as well as the soldiers until an immediate 'all hands' signal was issued stating 'Cease firing on B-17s coming towards you'. Within 10 minutes, the attackers had gone.

The eight B-17s which landed at Hickam on Sunday one of them was destroyed but the remaining seven were able to fly on the next day. (Recent research has revealed that eight B-17s came in at Hickam with two landing at

Haleiwa and one at Bellows and one at the Kahuku golf course.)

Wheeler Field

In the Wheeler Army airport Ray Carson, like so many others in the morning was thinking about breakfast. It was 7.55 am, he'd filled his tray before heading off to get a cup of coffee. Then, shocked by a huge explosion, he went outside the mess hall to see his red-colored balls from an Japanese plane whizz by at the speed of 75 feet. The plane's dark motive was highlighted by the enormous torpedo hung in a threatening position below its belly. He went to the barracks in order to take on the task however all that he could find was the 0.45 calibre gun.

Twenty-five dive bombers landed on the hangars. One bomb struck the barracks. After destroying the hangars planes circled around the airfield and then swarmed around the aircraft - the Japanese determinedly wiped out any chance of pursuit. After the planes had left, they left two hangars in ruins and the wreckage of more than two-thirds the planes at the base.

The death raged quickly on Wheeler Field. Mechanical engineer Leon DeKeyser was in his tent when the plane flew over. The airmen he was with were quick to leave to see the plane better. Within a moment, two people sitting next to him were thrown into the earth. "They were all shredded," the man recalled. Despite the danger the situation was, DeKeyser dragged the two corpses to the tent 'just to show respect'. In the tent, the sergeant was dead in his bunk bed. DeKeyser jumped under a mattress before lying still.

Six Wheeler's P-36 Hawk Fighters managed to fly up in the air. Of them four, four were involved in combat against nine Japanese aircraft, and later claimed two kills to compensate for losing just one Wheeler plane.

However, very little American planes were in the air during that time. Two lieutenants from Wheeler Field had their planes at Haleiwa. Despite playing all night at a poker table the two were wide awake to contact Haleiwa and request that the P-40s of their aircraft to be heated up. They then ran to Wheeler Field to the fighter strip, and took to the air around 8.15 am and were able to take down a Japanese aircraft.

Ford Island Naval Air Station

The Ford Island Naval Air Station radio operator Henry Read had finished his breakfast and was now able to resume his duties in Radio Shack. It was time to sort through messages that had been received from his previous shift ready to deliver them to the chief for the day at 8.00 am. "The next incident I heard was a huge explosion near Ford Island's South End of Ford Island and a geyser of water erupted in the air for hundreds of feet' he recalls. After that, he witnessed fighters flying over the planes and bombs dropping. There were people running to the safety of the drainage ditch that lies at the end of the runway. The Metalworker's duty officer in the shop came out and stated "Those are Japanese aircrafts. These scumbags are bombarding us!'

The three patrol squadrons on Ford Island on 7 December were in a good condition of readiness. Half the aircraft had four hours' notice, and ammunition and machine guns were present in all planes that were not being repaired. However, it was a level of state of readiness that didn't allow for an attack that had just four-hour notice.

The speed at the attack was able to strike was frightening. The moment the first explosion sounded, Ted LeBaron ran to the hangar, avoiding the shards of shrapnel that poured out. When he arrived at the hangar, almost all of the aircrafts were destroyed because of the fuel they had in their tanks. As the commander of the base reached his spot, the only thing he had to do was urge the crew to pull the planes that were not damaged away from the wreckage that was burning. However, in spite of all the confusion, the fire brigade arrived but they discovered that the Arizona was unable to connect to the water main after she landed at the bottom of the harbour. Ford Island was gushing with fuel but there wasn't an inch of water in sight.

In this chaos rolled an aircraft from the USS Enterprise. Captain H Hopping recalled that, when they ascended Barbers Point, he could see smoke. On the radio, he heard the voice of a man saying "Do not try to attack me. This is a six baker three American plane. The voice then went on to advise his gunner go out as the plane was sinking under the water. Hopping was able to land on Ford Island and later took off to re-discover the waters towards the West and west of Barbers Point.

Ewa Marine Air Station

Captain Leonard Ashwell, based at the Ewa Marine Air Station, was watching the planes come in. He was certain of them being Japanese and was rushing into the chaos, shouting "Air Raid". When the attack occurred, attack, a bugler was standing in front of him, ready to begin his new year. As he was getting ready to put his lips in his bugle spotted the planes, and shouted"Captain! These planes are Japanese war planes"The call to arms went out.

John Hughes ran to the barracks to warn the soldiers. Then he assisted in handing out ammunition for 1903 Springfield rifles which needed to battle planes. Hughes tried a couple of shots, but then decided to steer clear of the idea. He was determined to move the burning planes away from those unharmed. As the raid wore on, Hughes and his colleagues took pot-shots at Japanese and throwing flaming aircrafts towards the other side.

Of the 49 planes based at the field on that day, 33 were destroyed, and 16 were seriously damaged. There was not one plane left in good enough condition to fly.

Kaneohe Bay

The air strip of the naval located at Kaneohe Bay was also a major target for the morning. The attack took place just eight minutes after the Japanese aircraft landed at the harbor. As the nine fighters of the enemy arrived, they flew over the bay before they fled low, shooting the fire of machines guns. The first target they targeted was the four patrol planes moored on the ramp. As they crossed across the low shore, they made for the planes that were that were on the ramp.

Director Aviation ordnanceman John Finn wasn't even on the base when the assault arrived, but he ran into his vehicle as soon when he saw the planes approaching. When he got to the base, he discovered that the vast majority of the aircraft were in flames. The men around him attempted to bring the guns working by using pieces of scrap metal that were used to replace the mountings for guns that were missing. Finn did not care about their struggles and took a gun mounted on a mobile mount. In the open, Finn put up an 0.5-inch machine gun, and shot at planes. He remained there for two hours later , refusing to leave the area until the last plane of the enemy was been destroyed. After Finn was finally removed it was discovered that he had 21 shrapnel wounds as well as one foot was shot through by a bullet. After a quick patching at a hospital, Finn returned back to the base in order to prepare the remaining aircrafts for use. It was not surprising that Finn was given the Medal of Honour some months afterward.

The 36 PBY Catalina seaplanes at the base 27, 27 were destroyed in the area where they were stored. There was not a single plane operating. The only planes that survived were three that were on dawn air patrol during the attack. The third one was littered with bullet holes at the time it made its landing. One hanger was destroyed completely and all the records of service from squadrons 11-12 disappeared. (The records of squadron 14 remained.)

Bellows Field

Bellows Field was a prime instance of the fate which is awaiting military units who follow an established routine. On the 6th of December, it was a Saturday, and the base's twelve P-40s had just completed the practice mission. Like every other day, the planes were neatly parked without fuel and guns taken off. There was time to re-arm the plane on Sunday, and later on during the week, clean the guns and engines. But there was never the time. Wing-to-wing, the planes that were not used were made available to Japanese to use as they pleased.

The first incident was from one plane that was able to strike the area. A half hour later, nine Zeros appeared, possibly following an Air Force B-17 who had just arrived at the airport. However, Bellows Field was low on the list of Japanese priorities and was subject to less damage than other airfields. In spite of the state of preparation of the P-40s that were stationed at Bellows Field, three planes tried to take off. One pilot was hit by the Japanese Zero just before he was able to climb aboard his plane. The two other planes were able to get into the air, but fell before they reached any acceptable height.

The entire assault on the airfields took only ten or fifteen minutes. The piles of planes smoldering in the aprons as well as the mess of wrecked hangers, and join Fuchida as his aircrafts flew over the harbour that was sleeping.

Chapter 3: Smaller Vessels Take Over The Lead

The call to take action

The majority members of fleet officers as well as men were in the mainland during the raid. Initially, the men learned of the incident on the spur of the moment. A few saw planes flying hovering over Ford Island from their homes and others from the dock area, while others while visiting a ship. The first alert official was not issued until 7.58 at which point the announcement "AIR RAID Harbor. This is NOT a drill and was broadcast to all ships by the Lieutenant Commanding Logan Ramsay in Bellinger's office in Pearl Harbor. It wasn't till 8.04 AM that Honolulu radio broadcasted the message to all sailors to show up for duty. A minute later Kimmel arrived at his desk. While he was watching the unfolding drama, a single bullet flew through the window and struck Kimmel on the chest. He looked over to the Commander Maurice Curts, Pacific Fleet Communications Officer, who was at his side , and said "It would have been more lenient had it killed me.'

A lot of officers and men were unable to reach their vessels. In the Battleship Utah the commander and Executive Officer were also on shore leave,, so the responsibility for command fell to Lt. Commander Isquith. He proved to be competent and win the Navy Cross that day for the brave way the captain saved nearly 90% of the crew. The destroyer Blue went out to sea with only four officers, they were all junior and unexperienced officers. A junior lieutenant was required to be in charge of Wasmuth's destroyer in absence of her executive officer and commander. He succeeded in bringing the ship out safely from harbour.

Bagley is the pilot on the first flight of the day

Many ships were not in need of Ramsay's warning. Both men and officers were aware of the bombs dropping on Ford Island and smoke billowing across the sky. It was enough to call general areas. One of the first to enter actions were the destroyers Bagley. The Seaman Carl Otto recalled how he was eating an egg sandwich being on the gun mount following his mess shift , when an aircraft that he believed to be Chinese was hurling towards him. The pilot was seen waving. A torpedo then fell from the plane and smashed into Bagley that was moored in the destroyer pen. However, it wasn't intended to be used by Bagley. The torpedo reached the harbour before falling into battleship Oklahoma. General quarters Otto who was a powderman was shortly firing his gun of 5 inches, that was expected to use around 165 rounds during the day - but Otto always remembered the figure as being 300. He was trained for this particular moment, but then he said he had switched to automatic mode. On another weapon, chief Petty Officer Robert Coles, still chewing toast, was able to hack the locking mechanism of the 0.5-inch machine ammunition for guns.

Bagley claimed to have brought down six planes and was also privileged of having downed one of them. (Which was ironic, considering the fact that it was the intention of the military be protecting ships at anchor.) Two of the planes that arrived were able to pass over Bagley Bagley before she could get her guns. However, as the third plane torpedoed towards the capital ships , Chief of the Gunner's Squadron Harry Skinner fired. Skinner missed but struck the next plane directly and it sank to the bottom of the Harbour. Then the eighth plane that was en route arrived in Bagley's view. The plane turned around to escape the gunfire of the ship's machine guns however the Seaman Alphan Johnson caught it. The second fatality of the day vanished beneath the surface. As the fight heated up, an untrained seaman Lowe Peterson brought down Bagley's third plane, and it was thrown into the dockside crane. Two planes from the first wave soon fell to Bagley's mighty gunners.

The prompting of Avocet's AA

Another ship that was the first to go into combat included miningweeper Avocet. It was firing around 7.52 morning when they saw planes threatening the hangers of Ford Island. The victory came just a few minutes after when a B5N2 torpedo Bomber of the ship Kaga was moving away from its attack against the warship California. It was struck by the Avocet's

3 inch starboard gun. It it caught fire in mid-air and crashed into the areas of the hospital.

Tucker's early start

One man even managed to see the signal to the general quarters. Gunner's companion Walter Bowe on the destroyer Tucker observed the aircrafts of the enemy circling the harbour. The machine gun was fired prior to the time quartermaster Robert Burns had sounded the alarm. Within a few minutes, the guns that were 5-inches long were firing alongside those that of other destroyers within her fleet of ships. Two aircraft were hit with a flurry of shells and bullets. In the course of the day, Tucker was to score four dead Two of them blamed on Bowe on the machine gun.

Solace prepares for the possibility of casualties

Another ship that was in "action" but not into combat at the first hint warning of an assault was the medical ship Solace. The moment the sirens of air raids began to sound, the medical personnel and the seamen began to throw themselves into the chaos of restructuring that took place on board. Doors that were watertight were shut as were all cargo ports. Two gangways were open for rescuers to utilize. A 50-bed emergency ward was put up and all able-bodied patients were transferred to their respective ships. Patients suffering from burnt tonsils or painful hernias must remain in the waiting room. While the frenzied activity was taking place in the train, two Solace vessels were already on their journey to take in wounded of the Arizona.

10. Oklahoma's capsize

The best vessel to illustrate the speed and intensity of the assault as the Oklahoma. The old battleship that was lumbering - she was able to only achieve only 10 knots - was moored on Battleship Row on that fateful day. In front from her was Maryland however, it failed to protect Oklahoma Oklahoma from the looming disaster that was about to consume her. Just as the first planes appeared in view over the battleships three torpedoes struck her interior. The ship was able to turn within a matter of minutes.

Lieutenant Garth Brown, not yet dressed, was busy sanding his work with glee when the general quarters call rang out. In his underwear and apron, Brown was racing to get his station of battle in an ammunition magazine for one gun that measured 14 inches. Brown and his team took note of the people arriving. The last person to enter closed the hatch. The men were unable to observe the events their eyes could see the boat shake with each explosion , however in their quiet, there was a complete silence. The ship started to shake and the water began to flow into the ship. Then the PA system went off and the lights were turned off. In a state of incomprehensible communication with the outside world, Brown and his team members decided the time was right to go. By squeezing open a cloggcd and seldom used hatch, they were able to escape one at a time. The moment their feet get to the deck, they disappeared , sliding off the slippery and oily deck and into the water. There were a few who yelled for help the situation was as Brown remembered, "We couldn't see the water, so what should you do? You try for your own life.'

Private First Class Art Wells on Pennsylvania watched with awe as masts of Oklahoma's crippled masts moved toward the man. They moved down and down until they swam in the water. The keel of her came up and he could see the people spilling out of her decks, and sliding down the shiny the hull.

The Ensign Herbert Rommel was at one of the guns that fought on Oklahoma. As his troops were firing away in a desperate attempt to save the ship, Rommel was able to hear the sound of explosions emanating from the vessel's hull. He slipped through the turret to check if he was required to control damage. A second explosion followed immediately and caused him to flee back to the turret. In a matter of minutes, the growing number of ships caused him to be unable to operate the guns. Rommel left his post and tried to climb from a hatch in order to slip into the sea.

When the planes began to fly over , Seaman George Smith found himself in the 4th broadside, as well as three other recruits who were unsure how to operate the gun. As he looked out of an open porthole, he could not be believed when he saw torpedo bombers speeding toward the ship. There was a huge crash and the ship moved to the other side. The terror that flooded my heart was so intense that it was impossible to bear' said. In defiance of orders, and awed at the ever-growing list of demands of people, the soldiers sprinted from a porthole and sank into the water. While he struggled through the muddy water, he was sprayed by burning oil, Smith was looking back and saw the Oklahoma slide over.

The moment junior officer Adolph Mortensen heard the call to general quarters , he dressed in pyjamas. He was barely in to the boiler area when his ship crashed beneath him after the explosions of torpedoes. It was dark, and the ship began to drop. The ship then flipped over. and he was in the dispensary, the tiled floor is now up over his head. The area was filled with water, Mortensen as well as four other people were trapped in a shrinking air pocket. He swam down to find the knobs on the porthole that measured 11 inches. The porthole opened. Two people quickly walked through. Then came the steward who was in a bind. Mortensen handed him a massive shove. The ship's carpenter would be first, but he was aware that it was impossible for his 200 pound load could fit through the tiny porthole. The porthole was opened while Mortensen breathed a last breath of the exhausted air before diving. He emerged - however, he was not wearing his pyjamas.

In the case of some people, escape appeared impossible. Chaplain Aloysius Schmitt was in his station in the dressing area when the ship shook and started to roll. There was a frantic anxiety as a few men raced to close the door of the compartment. Schmitt calmly instructed the men and then sat down against the door, and then eased it into. The water was flowing through so quickly that it took only a few minutes for one sailor who was unconscious to be rescued and for a handful of men to hurry through before the entrance was blocked. There were only the portholes that were narrow to allow escape. Each time, the men squeaked through, but when one of them reached out to pick up Schmitt and he nodded his head. He was the highest-ranking person present; he'd be the last one to go. However, the waves came over the man before he was ready to leave.

Chapter 4: West Virginia Battles Fire And Flood

West Virginia suffered five hits from torpedoes as well as two 15-inch armor-piercing shells within just a few minutes. The first blast led to the deck's fall and, within minutes, all four casements, as well as the galley caught fire. The ship was fortunate with the speed at the way Captain Claude Ricketts, the assistant fire control officer, was in charge of fighting the flood. He snatched a man named Billingsley and they began to close hatches, shutters and doors. Then he spotted two more people, Rucker and Bobick, who were beginning to do some counter-flooding independently. He instructed them to flooding everything on the side facing the port. The list of ports soon diminished as did it was a matter of time before the West Virginia was righted. Ricketts was later acknowledged as stopping the ship from collapsing.

A lot of those on the West Virginia had no chance to be a part of any battle. When the baker Dale Augerson neared his battle station, the list of ship's men was so extensive that he was sent to the port side of the ship with hundreds of other crew members in order to counter the growing list of men.

Machinist Mate Johnnie Gner gazed at the burning sea and realized there was no way to escape via a the raft. After locating a calm area in the water, Egner jumped into the water and headed towards the dockside. The luck was with him when he emerged from the burning oil, and was saved by a tugboat passing by.

Seaman John Coffey was ordered to assist wounded soldiers out of the turret number 3. He climbed up the 12-foot ladder to the hatch and looked into the hatch. Inside, he saw the wounded and dead in a state of agony and a fire was going. With the assistance of another sailors, he carried a victim to the doorway holding an injured man on his back, Coffey made his way to the bottom of the ladder. When he stepped off his deck the injured man began crying that he was unable to see. After Coffey dropped his body into the motor launch and the gunwale was flooded, water hit the man's face. At when he shouted "I see. I'm sure you. It was then that Coffey remember that they were mess cooks in the same time as they used to get beef quarters from refrigerators on the ship for breakfasts for the crewmen.

The moment the Lieutenant Commanding D C Johnson arrived on the bridge that signals, he saw Captain Bennion wounded on the coffin. Lieutenant Commander Beattie was by the side of the captain when he was hit by shrapnel. The captain was swollen and fell groaning onto the deck, with a massive stomach wound. Beattie asked an assistant pharmacist to come to aid the captain and then he instructed Lieutenant Ricketts to be in charge of bringing the captain admitted to the hospital. Then, Johnson brought along the strong-built mess attendant Doris Miller. She carried the bunk all the way to the ladder, with the shifting and bumping was extremely difficult for Bennion. However, once they reached the top of the ladder , it became apparent that it was impossible to bring the cot off with an injured man. Bennion was scheduled to be killed at the top of his ladder.

Lieutenant Archie Kelley, an assistant damage control officer for the West Virginia, faced a decision that nobody wants to take, not even when it comes to obligation: to cause others to death. His first job during an emergency is to make sure closing of all water-tight doors. When he reached the central station located on the lower deck, he was able to find a door that wasn't shut. The water was pouring in. When he was attempting to shut the door, he got the sight of sailors entering the next compartment. His decision was easy to either wait for the sailors and then irreparably overflow the central station or shut the door. Kelley shut the door. He then turned to Commander Harper with a look which prompted a counter-order, should the officer wish. No counter-order came. In the back of the room Kelley was able to hear the screaming and screams of men fighting to escape. In the end, Kelley's reasoning was to be right. Four people died, but those at the central station were spared. They worked for about one hour at their positions until the oil and water reached their shoulders. Then they ran away through a tube that leads to the upper deck.

It was about 9.00 am at the time that Harper looked over the scene. The deck of the boat located on the port side of the vessel was submerged in water. The entire waterfront was filled with burning oil, with flames burning across the side facing the port of the ship. The captain was reluctant to send his men to be thrown into the boats. They were ordered to remain near the West Virginia until the last possible moment to save as many people as they could.

The rescue of wounded soldiers from West Virginia required heroic efforts. The commander Harper directed that the wounded be transported in blankets to the forecastle, from which they could be put into boats that were on one side. Lieutenant Commander Beattie was able to send a team of soldiers to investigate in the region of the forecastle. Then, a lot of wounded were brought out on the deck which was under fire from strafing. They were then lowered into boats , and then taken for

The Solace hospital ship as well as the Naval Hospital. While it was crucial to save the victims was Beattie decided not to cause more harm. He directed his men to be prepared when a plane was approaching. Lieutenant Commander Johnson also directed the removal of wounded. One of the ports on 5 inch gun cases, he discovered two severely injured men. They were piled onto benches - there was no stretchers on hand - and then laboriously trimmed from the gun casement. The floor was slick and slippery. Inside it was dark.

Some of the men did not get off. As the ship was about to be repaired, 70 bodies were discovered trapped in various spots. One of them was a calendar with dates that were crossed off. Last cross occurred made on 23 December.

12. Nevada's most wonderful escape

The Nevada general quarters, the sound was heard about 8.00 am. The commander Robertson who was worried about an attack from a surprise, had broken the law when he earlier directed that the ammunition boxes be filled to capacity and all guns kept in their positions of readiness. In the end, Nevada was among the first large ships to fire on that day, 2 minutes after 8 o'clock. One plane fell before it crashed down into the ocean. Despite the AA fire, a torpedo fired by another plane hit her Nevada on her bow to the port.

Woody Derby thought the call to general quarters was merely an exercise, regardless of the fact that Sunday was an unusual day. When he was five decks lower in the Nevada's magazine, and a request was made to request ammunition, he inquired if you want to practice with ammunition or do you need combat ammunition?' Only when the call came back with live rounds did Woody realise that something significant was taking place. How serious the matter wasn't apparent at first Woody when the magazines started to overflow. He was soon faced with no alternative than to flee his position and walk up a few floors to be part of a damage-control team. It wasn't until 4.30 after midnight did the officer venture to the open air and be able to see at first the smoldering wrecks that were circling him. The destruction to the Nevada was extensive and the largest hole in her hull measuring approximately 45' by 30. The bow portion of the vessel was damaged.

The Nevada was saved that day thanks to the quick actions from the Chief Officer Francis Thomas. The ship, which was moored in the middle of the fiery Arizona was in a dangerous location. He instructed the Nevada to begin its journey at the fastest speed possible. At 8.40 am, the ship was in motion despite having been hit by a torpedo as well as two or three bombs. A wary Japanese pilot saw the vessel moving and flew into the area to bomb it. The vessel was hit and started to absorb the water. Thomas recognized that he could be at risk of Nevada sinking into the channel, and he decided to shore her on Hospital Point.

Before that the Nevada was grounded, her gunners fired at three enemy aircraft - likely dive bombers. Crew members of Nevada watched while three planes crashed. One was in a field of cane towards Ewa and The Naval Hospital and the last in the channel.

After the Nevada was sunk, Thomas supervised her damage control for two days before ending as a tired man. Thomas's actions were not without notice and Thomas was given with the Navy Cross for having saved the Nevada despite heavy enemy bombing as well as strafing'. The Navy Cross was awarded to him for "excellent judgement' when putting the ship back on track and for keeping her on the ground in order to stop it from sinking.

Chapter 5: The Californian's Failure To Complete Its Mission

The most odd events of the assault was the sight of California's bandsmen standing on the deck just before 8.00 am waiting to play the colors. The first bomb that fell upon Ford Island without exploding her the band members were slightly shocked. When the next blast caused off the Ford Island hanger into the air, they knew that this was not a ordinary Sunday. A glimpse of the rising sun's symbol as well as the sound from general quarters sent musicians racing to their positions. The bandmaster John Rutledge never reached his after his 8.05 am torpedoes took his body off and into scorching water. He took a swim towards the slip of the ferry and climbed up the rope that was knotted to escape. Rutledge was taken to the photography lab and there was a K-20 aerial camera that contained fifty feet of film it was thrown into his hands. He set off to capture the scene for the next couple of hours. The film was shipped off to Washington which meant he didn't see the final images. It is highly probable that a lot of the photos of the wrecked ships we see today were shot by the photographer.

The electrician Linn in the California was in the process of eating breakfast when general quarters began to sound. A plane sporting rising sun's symbolism reflected through a porthole was sufficient for him to be sent post-haste into the control center. His task was to assist the California to sail off to sea in a matter of urgent need. He was just receiving the directive to change to the condition ZED when he heard sound of two torpedoes hitting the vessel. Despite the explosions the engines started as usual. The ship was soon prepared to leave the fire. The steam pressure started to fall. Within minutes , it was at a completely zero. In addition, there was seawater now within the oil fuel.

The torpedoes ripped the port side of a 40-foot hole. on the side facing port. Despite the initial listing the batteries of California's AA batteries were working within a couple of minutes, before another torpedo was sent home, this time taking out a hole of 27 feet wide by 32 feet.

The heroic efforts were undertaken to keep the guns in service. the guns, however they were shattered by the shortage of ammunition. Ensign Blair recruited ten soldiers to assist in getting some ammunition. The soldiers had no alternative but to reopen the now shut ZED hatches to access the weapons. Blair handed out 200 rounds of ammunition in belts for each of the men. With their load sagging, they climbed to on the ladders that surrounded the ship that was listed. Below, Blair continued to belt more ammunition. A rising leak of fuel oil made him climb up to the to the top. He loaded his troops with as much ammunition they could carry. He also gave orders to the machine for clipping to be lifted. It was never able to reach the deck, and when Blair returned to look the machine, he discovered the torpedo's hold completely flooded. On deck, the crew and Blair began to load the ammunition with their hands. They were able to only manage 100 rounds until the "abandon ship' sounded. Blair's efforts have assisted California to take one plane that was down in the early hours of 8.30 am. The plane crashed into the flames after being shot by machine guns. Another plane was reported to fall in the vicinity of Ford Island two minutes later likely due to the gunnery of California.

The men who were in the engine room in the forward soon found themselves in trouble after the second torpedo exploded. Smoke began to fill the room. The Ensign Lewis and his men shut off the ventilation systems and put on gas masks. The air was still smokey, and they discovered that the smoke was emanating from the painted walls in the room. A fire, which they were unable to see was burning. They found the position just when the call to evacuate the ship rang, when they discovered that the forward hatch was hot to even touch. Their efforts to open it went unsuccessful. Then it was released from the opposite side. Lewis and his crew swung to the left of the flame and returned to the deck to discover the ship completely abandoned.

John Madden, a radio man, turned his phobia of claustrophobia to his advantage in California when he was under decks in darkness with fellow seamen. He was lost. However, he learned the route in darkness as a way to get over his condition. Without the need for light the man led a group of people through the corridors and up ladders until they reached the rescue from the top deck.

The state of California was the site of two amazing sacrifices of self. In one point, the Forward Air Compressor was the Machinist's Mate, aged 25 years old Second Class Robert Scott. The compressed air was essential to the other crew members on the ship. A torpedo that struck nearby caused fuel and water oil pouring into his cabin. When the water reached waist-deep all of Scott's fellows were gone. They pleaded with Scott to come with them. Scott refused, crying to a gunner's friend "As long as I'm able to provide these people with air I'm going to stay.' Scott was never seen again, and was later given his Medal of Honour. Radio electrician Thomas Reeves fell in the similar manner. He was a part of a group that was distributing ammunition to the lower levels. The fire started in the corridor, but Reeves did not leave his position and was killed in the fumes and the flames.

14. Catastrophe affecting the Arizona

Nobody aboard the Arizona was prepared for the attack. When the Japanese aircraft roared toward her mooring point, Ensign Jim Miller was still dressing and Ensign Flannigan was not yet been dressed, as Lieutenant Commando S G Fuqua was eating his breakfast in the room for wards. The innocent plans for an unproductive Sunday were disrupted when the vessel sounded its Air Raid siren. This it was Ensign Davison who sounded the alarm. He was getting ready for the colours when he heard the sound of a dive bomber flying over. Through his telescope, he was able to see red dots appearing on the wings. This appeared to him as odd. After that, bombs began to fall over the airfield. Davison signaled the alarmand led captain Van Valkenburgh and Fuqua on the deck. The alarm was triggered at 7.55 am. Captain Davison walked straight to the bridge, and Fuqua directed Davison to sound the general quarters. At that moment , the first enemy aircrafts were flying over the ship. Fuqua was able to see that one plane glide over the Arizona around 100 feet. Then the first bomb was dropped. The blast sent Fuqua onto the deck, and he became unconscious. (Arizona was on the outer side of her mooring paired with Vestal, the ship for repair Vestal was hit with bombs instead of torpedoes.)

Miller woke up. Miller was alerted, He was not aware that the raid was taking place and he took a moment to change into his uniform prior to going down the third deck to inspect the doors. He was only able to get to on the 2nd deck. He came across an officer who was searching for keys to ammunition. Miller was off looking for the captain and the gunnery officer, but was unable to locate neither. He decided to give up his search and eventually made it into the 3rd deck. Another time, his attempt to look for doors was blocked again, this time due to general quarters sounding. Miller ran off to his position in an Turret. After Miller arrived at the unharmed turret 3, he rang on the phone and spoke to the plotters. He discovered that there was no other turret in line. The only thing he could do was sit and wait. In a flash the turret was shaken up by an explosion, but there was no harm had occurred. After that, Arizona's colossal explosion as her magazine exploded up. The phone went out of service. Smoke was escaping from the hatch that was open. All Miller saw was the wall of fire. He emerged from the turret and saw an array of small burning bodies scattered all over, and a seriously hurt Ensign Anderson. In the absence of power and with the atmosphere suffocating with fumes, Miller saw that the turret wasn't going to work that day, and ordered his troops to be brought on deck to battle the flames. In the deck's main area Ensign Davison was there, and was the one who had to maintain the general quarters in a safe manner, noticed an explosive strike the deck with the turret 4. He grabbed every man that he could see, and then set the task of removing off the hoses.

Lieutenant Hein took off from the Mess for junior officers at the general quarters' sounding and headed for the deck of the boat. He took the time to notice that the AA guns on the port side were operating. When he went over to the signal bridge and was told that he was not required, so he walked to the navigation bridge in which he found the quartermaster and captain. Before he could get any instructions the bridge was shaken by a huge explosion. Fire poured through the shattered windows. Three men raced to the port door however, they discovered it was closed. They then headed for the starboard entrance. Hein fell and tripped on the deck. He woke up and discovered that the port's door was open. Fighting through flames and smoke, He climbed down into the signal bridge, and got to the deck of the boat by leaping off the messy mess of the ladder for the signal bridge. There was no trace of the captain or quartermaster has ever been found. The blast also claimed another important casualty of high rank: Rear-Admiral Isaac Kidd, Commander of Battleship Division 1 and was last seen at the signal bridge.

Seaman Donald Stratton was in the port AA director's office up the foremast during the moment when the Arizona explosion. The moment the bomb hit the ship , it'shook as if it was shaking according to him. There was a huge explosion that lifted the ship almost from in the ocean'. It was followed by an inferno that reached 500-600 feet in the air. The foremast of the ship was consumed by fire, as was the entire bow of the vessel.

Attack on the Arizona occurred so quickly that the majority of the crew were given no chance of manning their positions. Most of the injured men were enlisted to fight fire or in the process of evacuating wounded. If Fuqua - the man who at that time was then the highest officer in charge of deciding to issue instructions - became conscious, it was to a disorienting noise of AA fire. an inferno between the ships and in the aft area of the ship submerged. It was impossible to find pressure on the mains of the fire, and Fuqua instructed Davison to contact to the engine room. The pressure did not come on and the men battled the flames using buckets of liquid and fire extinguishers made of CO_2. However, the situation was not a good one. The oil was leaking onto the deck, and the sea was coated with burning fuel.

When the flames started to rage then the focus was switched to the evacuation of injured people at the dock side as well as to Solace. Davison along with Ensign Bush were able to take three boats and pulled them out of the scorching sea to save men who had jumped into the sea. They carried boatload after boatload of injured and burned men to the docks at Ford Island. Then Bush was able to launch boats alongside the Arizona to retrieve one of the men that had fallen off the stern of the boat. In his account, Bush noted that Davison's heroic task was completed despite having been badly burned.

When the time was right to go to the dock, Seaman Donald Stratton and his mates could climb the ladder - which was a sure death. A sailor from the Vestal, Joe George, helped them out. He threw out a heaving line with a heavier one attached to the platform for controlling the sky. One by one, the men crossed hand-in-hand along the line until they reached the Vestal. Six men crossed the line and were all severely burned. Stratton suffered from 50 to 60 percent burns. He was for the next nine months in the hospital.

Many men fell to their deaths in the flames of the debris. Others, initially trapped managed to escape successfully. Ensign Flannigan was taken to the lower part of the turret as general quarters began to sound. He was standing on the top of the ladder, when the bomb that hit between turrets 3, and 4 shut down all light sources. The lower area of the turret was soon filled with toxic gasses. The first thought of Flannigan was to take the men out of the passageway that runs between turrets 3 and 4 but the door was blocked. They then tried to isolate themselves in the lower area. After closing the passageway to one door, they were thwarted by the doors to the next. There were numerous attempts to contact for assistance, however neither the main telephones as well as the sound-operated ones worked. As the smoke grew stronger and the water started rising in the room , the men were forced to make a choice: they'd have to find a way to get out through the hatches leading up through the turret. With great difficulty , they opened the hatches to open, and then climbed the smoke-filled decks and onto the main deck, which was blazing hot. They swiftly shut all hatches that were behind them. The day of Flannigan's work was not finished but. He was busy taking injured people to the dock until he was able to deliver the final boatload of the day.

Chapter 6: Maryland's Fortunate Escape

One of the less damaged battleships of the time was Maryland. It was also one of the few vessels that several guns in her arsenal during the attack. One of these guns was where the gunner's mate Leslie Short, sat writing the letter. When he heard the alarm, the man dropped his pen and paper, picked up his machine gun, and quickly started firing at two torpedo planes which were coming towards the eastern part of. Both planes had already dropped their weapons, but Short was determined to do not cause any more harm on in the same day. When he struck the first plane, it emitted flames and smoke before veering away from the hospital base after it rapidly fell in height. Short thought he destroyed the second plane however, said, 'I was so busy, I'm not able to confirm it'. The commander however acknowledged two deaths to him in his after-battle Action Report.

It was also the site of a narrow escape. Maryland is also site of one of the small escapes during the day. George Williams had slept on the deck that night. He awoke around 7.00 am, unrolled his cot and carried it down to the bed. A half hour later, the bomb exploded two feet from his bed. He was proud of himself for getting up early.

While the Maryland was hit by two bombs, she continued her AA fire. She even sent firefighting teams to ships that were more affected than she. However, the Maryland was surely in a state of chaos since Japanese pilots mistook her as sinking.

16. Utah - the ship that was targeted that was able to live up to her name.

It was just one minute after eight on the warship Utah and the colors were just being raised. When the ship was struck by an enormous explosion caused by an torpedo strike and she began to list her way to port. Then, a second torpedo hit the ship and the list grew up to fifteen degrees. The signal was heard "All hands on deck, as well as all engines room and radios, fire rooms, and dynamo watches to be laid down on the deck and free all prisoners. The deck below Robert Swift was busy doing his Christmas cards for his family members in Tennessee when there was a lot of noise from the top of the ship. He rushed up towards the upper deck, and shook his head in shock at dead sailors lying on the deck.

As a target vessel, the Utah was unable to withstand the assault since all of her guns, including her 5-inch and 1-inch ones were covered in steel housing. Machine guns were removed and placed beneath decks. The ammunition was stored in safe magazines.

One of the consequences of having a targeted practice status was that her deck was clad by two layers of timbers measuring 6-inches by 1-inches. Once the ship started to list, the blocks began to shift. The crew members who were trying to get off the ship were crushed as blocks fell apart and crashed into them. However, the crew member Aubrey Mahaney was lucky. He was able to make it to the other side before sliding to the bottom of the oily waters. He was terribly smashed from the rough barnacles that clung to the boat, but it was his only wound of the conflict. While he and other survivors made their way towards the dock, enemy planes continued to bombard them. One after another disappeared under the surface. After landing, Mahaney plunged into a pit, along with some men in deep shock. A lieutenant later appeared and instructed the men to put up the machine gun. They started however, as Mahaney said"the sights and sounds of defeat were everywhere in the air ... it was sick'.

Clark Simmons, together with two officers, heard the abandon ship call and sought ways to escape. The most convenient way to escape was through the captain's cabin that was equipped with three portholes of 18 inches. They were big enough for men to pass through, but they were not equipped with their life jackets. In removing their jackets, they made their way to the deck with an upward angle of 45 degrees. As they did, the ship reached its tipping point. When she started to sink, the three men slipped into the ocean and went towards Ford Island.

Seaman Truett Davis was able to recall the horror of the Utah's final moments. He was able to climb the top of the deck using a ladder that was accessed to the officer's wardroom. He could feel his mooring line snapping and under the feet of the soldiers, the deck's timbers bounced and hurtled. From above, he could hear the strafing of aircrafts of the enemy. There was no time to make an elegant exit: Davis plunged into the boiling waters and escaped.

Some people gave up the chance to escape to ensure that the power, boilers and lights on until as long as is possible and also to minimize the risk of any further explosions. Chief water-tender Peter Tomich was still at his job when the water were closing in on him. Tomich had come to America in 1913. USA in 1913. He enlisted with the Army in 1917, and was later a navy officer. Tomich died in the year 1913 and was awarded the Medal of Honour for 'extraordinary determination and disregard for his security'.

One particular man was nearly unable to exit the vessel The name of the man was Commander Isquith. He was just about to tour the vessel to ensure that there were no people to be rescued (excluding those who were trapped inside the ship's interior). At 8.12 am, Utah's mooring lines started to snap. She was swaying over. Isquith tried to open the escape escape hole - it was closed. His only option was a porthole for which he had to sit on the table. He moved a table into the spot, hung it up and started to let it out. The table then slipped from under him. Isquith was caught between death and life. A strong hand grasped the only arm he passed through the porthole and pulled. Isquith could be saved.

Utah was abandoned, her hull turned upside down and a number of men in the. The commander Isquith was among the first to notice the sound. He yelled for a torch to cut through the Raleigh and his crew began to do the work on the hull as the Japanese planes flew over the aircraft from above. Machinist S A Szymanski, Chief Machinist's Mate Terrance

Macselwiney, and two seamen rescued 10 of the sailors who were buried.

The last person to be removed was fireman Jack Vaessen. He had an amazing story to relate. He was on deck when he heard an enormous sound and then felt the vessel being swept over. He didn't know what had transpired and was left in the darkness with only an open flame and a dog wrench to assist in closing and opening watertight doors. When the water began to rise, he made his way to a different room, and shut the door that was watertight behind him. Every when the water rose, it was repeated until he came to the point of no return. It was a good day for him because he was just under the place where the cutters were working.

17. The Tennessee is trapped Tennessee

In the Battleship Tennessee Frank Curre was mess cooking at 8.00 am. There was a loud blast, which was quickly followed by another, even larger one. When he got on deck, he was stunned by the 'first terrible image I've ever seen The stricken Arizona. The request for general quarters was made and the doors to the Tennessee's watertight were shut. The Tennessee's AA fired up with fire as instructions to evacuate were sent into the room for engines. The steam pressure began rise.

However, Tennessee was in a bind. In front of her was the overturned Oklahoma. To her port, was her West Virginia, now settled on the bottom, pushing Tennessee to the side of dock. To the left there was also on the other side was Arizona with her leaking fuel tanks. The smoke and flames nearly destroyed the ship. Tennessee was soon enveloped by an incense-smelling cloud, which took all oxygen out of the air.

It was in the state of Tennessee was struck by two bombs of the second wave about 8.30 am. One of them destroyed the catapult and damaged the turret 3 badly. The other struck Turret 2. (It came from a fragment of the hit that fatally injured Captain Bennion, the captain of the West Virginia.) Tennessee was not seriously injured, but she was threatened by the fire of Arizona. The flaming fragments fell down the Tennessee. All efforts were devoted to fighting fires. The worst was gone at 10.30 am, however Arizona continued to be a risk for the next two days.

18. Pennsylvania's light penalty

The Pennsylvania did not suffer the first wave attack, but at 9.06 am, a 500-pound bomb from a plane at high altitude struck her boat's deck as she lay on the dry dock. One of her guns, which measured 5 inches, was struck and instantly killed the entire crew. A half hour later, an explosive hit the dock and shut off lighting and power to Pennsylvania. The main water pressure also was cut. Art Wells found himself trapped in an area between two casements at the time the first bomb exploded. As he slipped and slid through consciousness, he was a little aware of the hordes of men in the casement 7. They were like a nest of squirming worms ' as they tried to unravel' He remembered. He realized that there was a pile of people beneath him. He felt the weight of the pile and the warmth of the men over him. Unable to get his bearings, He suddenly felt the weight gone, and a hand taking him away from the living pile.

Pennsylvania did not suffer any further major harm, despite a plane continuing to carry out strafing attacks fifteen hours after it hit her. After the war, her machine shields were discovered to have been hit 30 times, but not a single bullet penetrated them. Then her guns smashed into the plane, and it crashed on hospital grounds. The commander declared the killing a 'certain' kill, while his men claimed five planes that were shot down. The woman was certainly hard to beat that day with her weapons, having fired 350 rounds of 5-inch ammunition and 350 rounds of 3-inch along with 60,000 rounds 0.5-inch ammunition.

Chapter 7: Other Heroes From The Time

A number of other ships were also attacked that day. They were mostly to be, for the Japanese simply small fry that were in the wrong spot at the wrong time.

Raleigh was saved from capsize

The time was 7.55 am when Seaman Pat Duncan stood on the deck of the destroyer Raleigh looking forward to the dawn of the new day. At once, Japanese planes came across the deck and opened fire on vessels around. The Raleigh's deck was sprayed with water. deck. "Sound general quarters," said the officer of the deck. Duncan raised his bugle to his mouth and then blew. Silence. The bugle was swollen with water. He pulled out the instrument, and a loud as well as clear sound sent around 450 people running to their posts.

Shortly after the assault was underway, the Raleigh was struck by a 3-inch AA and 0.5-inch machine guns in action, hit by the torpedo. It pierced the ground to the fire room 2. Within minutes, she began to lean towards port. The possibility of capsize was imminent. The men rushed to remove everything they could off the deck. The first thing to go was the planes, that had to be lowered using hand power. The job was so neatly completed that they were then towed over the water and then reported to duty on Ford Island. The torpedoes (warheads taken away) were next and were followed by torpedo tubes, two catapults, and finally an iron cargo boom. The boat skids, stanchions as well as life rafts and booms were also deposited in the harbour, along with anchors. In the meantime, the counter-flooding was being initiated. The commander R E Simons was done "to perfection". This heroic effort have saved this Raleigh and she was in a position to serve sandwiches and coffee to her crew members at their stations.

New Orleans praises the Lord

The large cruiser New Orleans was in one of the repair docks when her crew observed enemy planes hovering in the vicinity of Ford Island at 7.57 am. The general quarters were immediately notified. Soon after, the ship was under attack by dive bombers. Her engines were being rebuilt and all light and power came from the dockside. The target was sitting however, with the advantage that she had a wall along her port side, and an oiler Ramapo on the starboard side. In front of her were three destroyers, and on her bow on the starboard side is the tender for destroyers Rigel. There was no danger of being hit by a torpedo as she was restricted. The first two bombs fell on the waters, one in front and one behind the Rigel, without explosion. The third bomb burst into the dock's water in the area between Rigel along with The New Orleans. A cannonade made of metal fragments hit the two ships, causing severe damage to the superstructure and hull of both.

On deck, all the batteries from the AA battery were active within a matter of 10 minutes, even when they were to be handled with a hand. While Chaplain Howell Forgy watched the soldiers swunging the shells from one place to another along the long chain towards the deck, he called out , 'Praise God and release all the guns.' (This cry later was the inspiration for Frank Loesser to write the popular wartime tune that has the same name.) All the crew members on board New Orleans put up a vigorous defense, particularly considering their inexperience. 40 percent of the men not had any training in gunnery and, as the ship was in the process of being repaired and was in repair, there was no targets practice for the past about six months.

Phoenix is able to whack the angry bees

On the morning of the light cruiser Phoenix Commander Ted Hechler was woken up by the squealing sounds of the klaxon as well as voices yelling 'All hands general quarters'. Before he could get himself out of the bunk, the loud message was changed to 'Man the antiaircraft battery. This isn't drill! It's not an exercise!' He was reminded that those words were repeated repeatedly over and over again 'almost imploringly'.

Hechler quickly reached the gun batteries, and the awnings were up following a recent inspection conducted by Admiral. The crew swiftly took off the awnings, took out to the guns, and then opened the locks on ammunition storage boxes. Hechler and his men faced an uphill climb. The guns were not able to fire. the guns could be fired under the control of an automatic system - the Japanese planes were just too close. Every gun had to be left on its own to shoot and aim as best as it could. The distance and speed of the planes made it impossible to achieve precision aiming, and the gunners set up an entire wall of fire which they hoped that the planes would take off. Hechler said the experience was like trying to take out the bees in a rage within the confines of the phone booth'.

Hechler was able to get a close glimpse of the destruction of a Japanese aircraft. The pilot had rushed into the area the air and shot his torpedo. When he walked towards the Phoenix He banked to make a turn and was sucked into a torrent of shots fired by the gunships of the ship. The plane caught fire and then flipped on its back , then crashed into the seaplane delicate Curtiss just five minutes after nine.

There were no casualties in the crash of Curtiss as the fire was was put out by the quick intervention of Sergeant G K Nicodemus.

Helena overcomes the flood

The Lieutenant C O Cook was one of the men aboard the cruiser Helena which had breakfast disrupted by the air raid. He was just entering the wardroom, when the warning arrived. The alert came as Cook approached the main deck, his cruiser went through a massive explosion. It appeared that she was lifted out of the ground and the lights were turned off. The Helena was struck amidships by a torpedo which was passing beneath the minesweeper Oglala that was anchored alongside her. (It may be possible the torpedo was aimed to hit Pennsylvania because Helena was in Oglala's usual berth on that day. Light cruisers weren't an ideal target for Japanese. Japanese.)

The Ensign Miller was running behind in the upper decks at the moment. He was able to feel the ship lift several feet up beneath his feet. The sky above him observed what he believed as seven aircraft dropping bombs towards the ships at a height between 50 and 75 feet. He then went to the bottom and found the store on the ship's wrecked and dead bodies scattered around and a blaze raging. He ran to the fire main but was disappointed to discover that it was not under pressure. With the assistance of two others, they dragged a hose down to the dockyard, and then hooked it with the supply of water. When they returned to the storeroom, they discovered that the fire was out, but the space was filled with water. Conscient that the danger to the ship's safety was the raging the water Miller examined the boiler room, engine room, and the diesel room. The rooms were all flooding rapidly. He discovered a submersible pumps along alongside chief machinist Jones they began to draw the water in the Diesel Room. In another area, a repair crew was busy sealing the leaks. The Helena did not suffer.

The entire harbour was filled with men who were trapped in hulls with a sloping top or behind doors that were watertight. Some were lucky enough be saved. On the night of Helena chief machinist David Jones battled his way through the smoke into the engine room ahead to see if there was any people there. He walked through one of the doors that were watertight and found eight men, of which six had already died. He helped two others to escape through the deadly smoke.

Vestal swerves away from danger

The ship for repair Vestal was anchored on the side of the port of Arizona during the attack. Within minutes of the initial planes arriving, Arizona was inaccessible to the assistance of any repairmen and the Vestal was in danger from the fires of the battleship. The Vestal was also harmed by the subsequent explosion in Arizona. As it happened, Vestal's 3 inch gun was jammed, and the gun crew was trying to get rid of the obstruction. The blast of the Arizona shot shattered the entire gun crew to the ocean.

However, Vestal was not without her problems. About five minutes past eight, two bombs -

likely to be targeted to be used in Arizona - came at her. The bomb on her port side fell three decks down towards the store, and there it was exploded. The fires broke out, requiring an immediate flood of the shop to shield the adjacent magazine. Another bomb destroyed the port side of the vessel, tearing between the woodworking as well as the shops-fitting zones. The force of the explosive that it exploded from the ship's bottom leaving a 5-foot hole in size.

Paul Urdzik remembered the engine room, which was filled with water following the bombing. The bulkheads were bent inwards and the water was pouring in. The damage control team arrived quickly to begin building up the damaged bulkheads in order to protect engines. The men, according to Urdzik were the 'unknown heroes that day.

At 8.25 am, Vestal's command structure was falling to pieces and communication with the topside were no longer functioning. The Chief Engineer dispatched an engineer up to investigate what was happening. He returned to inform "Sir, they're abandoning the ship'. The engineer responded 'Let's leave this place. Once on deck, they heard the PA blasting out "All hands return at your stations of battle, and get ready for the start of. A mere twenty minutes later with only her engines for steering The Vestal was moving.

The ship struggled to move forward before crashing to port and taking on water in the aft. The ship sailed for about 1100 yards of distance before getting away from the fire danger. But the soundings indicated that she was sinking deeper into the waters. Commander Young took the decision to bring her down before it got too late. At 10.00 am, the Vestal was safe in eleven feet of water. Young was honoured for his actions on that day. Young was awarded the Medal of Honour.

Medusa takes out another submerged midget

The Vestal was not the only repair vessel to take part in the day. The 10,500-ton Medusa was anchored at the entry point into the Middle Loch, well away from the main battle however, there were numerous destroyers moored along the port of her vessel. It was around 8.15 am, after the battleships had been battered, two fighters plunged into the loch towards her. The Medusa's 3-inch AA split the plane in two, and the other sank into the lake. The bombs had not been released.

About a half an hour after, the Medusa saw a periscope on her port side as well as to the right of Curtiss. She fired and was immediately followed by the guns of the Curtiss. The bullets bouncing off the tower's protruding top were evident, however the submarine was to be unharmed. Then, the destroyer Monaghan was seen, moving at 15 knots toward the enemy. Medusa and Curtiss were not firing while the Monaghan began to prepare for the fight. As she walked over the area in which the submarine last been seen , the Monaghan fired two charges of depth. The first charge was enough. A massive spout of black water shot up to the sky.

Shaw's stunning explosion

Another of smaller ships included the wrecker Shaw located in a floating dry dock just a few miles from Hospital Point. From 7.55 between

7.55 and 9.15 am, she was struck by three explosives containing liquids. The first two struck an area on the gun's platform, and went through the gun shelter platform, forecastle , and the main deck. The bombs appear to have detonated in the mess room of the crew on the platform's first deck. Another bomb that entered with an angle passed across the entire radio area, along with the front side of the stores office, and the office of supplies. The bomb finally exploded at the deck level before falling into the ocean.

The fires immediately erupted from the incendiaries as well as Shaw's fuel tanks that had ruptured. After a short time, the magazine was raised, and the bow tore away from the bow, until it became tacked to the Keel. (The photo that was taken of Shaw's huge explosion has become an famous photographs from the time.) At this point, the dry dock was sinking, and as the rising water rose, the bow of Shaw was slashed and vanished. At 9.25 am, the battle was lost when the flames began to rage in uncontrollable flames. The ship was ordered to leave the ship.

Wasmuth is able to escape

Shaw's comrade in arms Wasmuth, the destroyer did better. Wasmuth was part of a nest of eight vessels near the point of entry of Middle Loch. The close proximity of the others vessels made it so that just two of her guns could shoot. However, the ship scored many hits on planes of enemy in the second wave of attack in the early hours of 9.25 am. The crew in her engine room was gaining steam and by 9.32 am, the Wasmuth was successful in making it to the watch the channel's entrance from the outside.

Blue's heroic ensign

The most impressive events during the time was the operation that took place aboard the destroyer Blue. The nominal number of her crew was 158. However, she went out to sea on December 7 with just four officers aboard - the ensigns were all extremely inexperienced: N F Asher, I Moldafsky, J P Wolfe and R S Scott. In the period between 8.05 and 8.47 in the morning, the Blue was stationed within the East Loch and was firing her 0.5-ins and 5-inch guns. The unmanned destroyer's performance was one of the most impressive that day. The gun she used destroyed a potential four planes. Two were deemed to be definite killings, one of them crashing into an area and another into the seaplane soft Curtiss.

At 8.07 am, the engine room was instructed to get steam up for departure and the repair team started to get the vessel to go into action. The moorings crew were waiting, ready to quickly slip the ropes at the time of instruction. In 8.47 at the time of writing, Blue was on the move and was moving towards the channel that leads to the entrance. At 9.10 am, she was out in open sea patrolling. A half hour later, Blue found a submarine in underwater sounds. She dropped 4 depth charges. The sounds continued until Blue dropped two more charges. This time , a 200-foot stretch of air and oil bubbles erupted to the surface. Four planes and a submarine were a remarkable feat for a tiny and sub-manned vessel.

Helm struggles to get towards the open ocean

The wrecker Helm was among the few vessels that were moving around the harbour during the attack. When Captain C E Carroll heard the alarm for the air raid, he ordered the crew to her guns and pushed her Helm to the West Loch Channel towards the sea. It was too late to let the two boats of the ship on the water. They were then left to follow.

As the Helm moved forward, enemy planes were coming in from the ocean in pursuit of the large ships. They struck the Helm as they flew close to her and not a single bullet struck the ship. If the planes had landed within a couple of minutes, Helm could have responded by firing her machine guns. However, at the time the gun crew was still taking off their heavy grease for preservatives. But they were ready to fire at 8.05 am, and the A guns were fired two minutes after that. Within three minutes of beginning to start firing, Helm hit a plane that was coming towards the southwest. The plane crashed, caught fire, and crashed against some plants located in the Hickam Field area.

Around 8.20 at night, Helm was able to spot a conning tower close to the entrance of the channel. The boat seemed to be sitting on a ledge of rock with breakers running over it. Helm fired multiple times. There were splashes but the submarine fell off the edge, and vanished. In 8.30 am, the Helm was patrolling near the entrance to the harbour, and she again encountered an aircraft. The plane swerved away sharply probably due to being struck.

In the latter moments of the battle In the latter stages of the battle, Japanese aircraft had enough time and ammunition to shift their focus towards smaller targets. The Helm was one of them. It was 9.15 am, a plane of the fighter flew over the ship and dropped two bombs on her bow on the starboard side. The helm was swung over to port, while the boat was rolling and rocking while the machine gunners fired firing. The bombs landed harmlessly in the water, however the gunners' focus was disturbed by the twist and the plane sailed away without injury. It happened that just at the time when the bombs fell, Helm had just finished the repairs on her steering. The blast explosions again threw off her electrical systems. Her steering was lost, as were the sound system, repeaters and echo rangers. At 9.30 Helm had regained power and resumed her patrol without another incident.

Doomed Cassin and Downes

The two destroyers made up those who were victims from the second wave of attack. Two destroyers were among the victims of this wave attack. Cassin along with the Downes were lying next to one another in an empty dock. On the Cassin the commander Shea was eating breakfast while the Gunner's Mate E L James rushed into the corridor screaming 'Captain they're here, bombarding Hickam Field.'

A few minutes later, the dockside commander decided to fill the docks that were dry. Commander Shea was approached to shut down his vessel. It was too late to finish the task in a timely manner however his crew was successful in shutting the ship down starting from lower levels up. They had to cut through power cables that ran between compartments, and then disconnect all the portable blowers which were cooling the vessel. At 8.30 am, the task was complete. (It is not known if the work was ever completed.) Around 8.50 am, an explosive bomb exploded in the neighbouring Downes and Cassin exploded into a firestorm. Cassin was immediately overwhelmed by her neighbor's explosion of fire. Her crew evacuated the ship and set out in a desperate search of the dockyard's hoses. Within minutes, half of them were operating. Shea instructed his men to ensure that the hoses were on the torpedo and depth charges tubes, for fear that they could explode - He could see the torpedo warheads disappearing from the tubes that propelled them. The troops were regularly sprayed with burning debris , and occasionally, blasts and flying debris caused the hoses to fall out of their hands. Their perseverance paid off when the fire was brought under control around 10.45 am. At that point, the Cassin had fallen off of her keel blocks, and was leaning against Downes. It was believed that she was an irreparable wreck, however, she was able to be saved.

The Japanese quit Japan

The majority of Japanese aircraft had left before 9.30 at night. The battle cry as well as the thunder of AA guns, and the roar of aeroplane engines ceased and a quiet peace settled over the area. Incredulous, confused and furious they prepared themselves for the next assault. But it never happened.

An invasion, which was never took place

The widely anticipated invasion actually happen. There had been many reported sightings of invading paratroopers as well as landings on the same day. Kaneohe was among the many spots on the island that reports of an effective Japanese invasion were believed to be true. After hearing that parachutists of the enemy were wearing the dungarees of Japanese soldiers, Martin immediately ordered the men to dress in white. The whites first had have to get stained. Since there was no dye available an enormous mug of coffee was needed.

In Schofield Barracks the men were informed that the Japanese arrived and were wearing gray uniforms that had a red stripe across the legs. The men were told to put together complete field packs with live ammunition. With no breakfast, they were sent to the sugar cane fields. While in the fields equipped with his gun in place Frank Arellano heard the endless creaking of the dry leaves on the cane ready for harvest. Was it wind or the imminent adversary? Arellano was in the field for the entire night.

Chapter 8: Nagumo Decides

On Nagumo's carrier it was time to think about what his future plans were. After the planes returned from their missions, the airmen were confident that they would soon be back in the air to launch a third attack. However, when Fuchida was summoned on the bridge at Akagi to meet Nagumo, he saw Nagumo looking sombre. Nagumo asked him questions regarding the vessels that were sunk or damaged and also the state of the Oahu AA defences. The first two attacks had been simple, but would it be that easy in a third attack? There were plenty of reasons to not making the third strike. In Oahu this second attack of attacks had suffered a hefty AA attack from the ground, the fact that there was no American aircraft in the air. There were twenty planes destroyed on the second round, compared to eight lost in the first, there is every reason to believe that there will be more losses in the next wave. But it was also certain that every attack would result in a declining amount of damage: the most dangerous targets were long gone.

There was also the issue of American carriers. They would by now have heard about the attack and be in search of their Japanese fleet. If Nagumo continued to remain where he was, it would be necessary to arm his aircrafts and be prepared to strike American carriers. American carriers. These worries were made worse by the changing weather patterns that made deck conditions dangerous for both humans as well as machines.

Nagumo decided. There was the third wave not be there. He ordered the cessation of preparation of the planes. The planes were scheduled to go back to Japan.

They were devastated. They were aware that they might be causing more damage on Pearl Harbor - particularly to the fuel depots - and they believed they left an unfinished job. Nagumo's choice remains controversial until the present day. While it's difficult to know what would have transpired had Nagumo returned, we can be more certain of the implications of having not returned. Yamamoto's massive raid caused immense destruction to American battleships - vessels that were of no strategic significance. However, he was able to leave his Pacific Fleet with its most important resources: the men and tanks, fuel stations, submarines, and carriers. They were essential for every Pacific operations. If the fuel depots were destroyed the fleet would have been forced to depart Pearl Harbor and return to mainland ports. The carriers, which formed the backbone for American military power throughout the Pacific weren't damaged. In failing to cause serious damage to the resources of these carriers, Yamamoto has succeeded in upset the American population, but left them with the tools of attack.

21. America is awash in cost

American losses

When Kimmel and Short received report after report from Oahu's vessels and airfields. The cost of their recklessness was shocking. There were 2403 American servicemen had perished on the beaches of Pearl Harbor and a further 1178 were injured. (The Navy dead (2008) was much higher than that of Army (218).) When the attack Oahu had boasted of 301 aircraft, including 60 Scout bombers - planes that ought to have been operational in the early morning of 7 December. When the Japanese troops left, their air bases, the commanders added the remaining aircraft only 52 planes that could be used which included 11 patrol planes as well as 14 Scout bombers.

Of the eight battleships in the fleet four were sunk or had capsized (Arizona, California, Oklahoma and West Virginia). The other four suffered massive torpedo and bomb damage that, in the instance of Nevada was grave. (Yet it was only Arizona and Oklahoma were not salvageable.) There was a lot of injuries to two cruisers, Helena as well as Raleigh. Another cruiser, the Honolulu had been able to get off much more easily. Two of the destroyers Cassin as well as Downes, were completely damaged The Shaw was afflicted with non-mortal damage. Also, there was the possibility of damage to vessels that were used as auxiliary vessels. In total, 19 vessels were damaged or damaged, by fire or debris from ships adjacent to them.

Japanese losses

It was a small amount of Japanese losses were small The Japanese lost only 29 planes, along with six submarines (of five of which were midget submarines) had been destroyed. 55 airmen had suffered fatal injuries, along with nine midget submarines. There were unidentified losses on the other submarine that was sunk. More than 100 airplanes had been damaged. However, it was a tiny cost to compensate for the immense damage caused to the Pacific Fleet and the island's defenses. The Japanese were happy enough with their victory to continue their advance to Malaya, Thailand, Hong Kong and the Philippines in the days after the attack. In January 1942, the Dutch East Indies, New Guinea and the Solomon Islands were added to the list.

The success of Yamamoto

In the short-term, Yamamoto may be content by the performance of his troops and equipment. The altered bombs, torpedoes and explosives been successful. Training of his pilots in the new techniques of low-level torpedo as well as bomb attack was successful. The fleet was able to traverse miles of ocean and had mastered the art of refueling while steaming. Most importantly, secretive diplomacy and deceit in planning had resulted in complete delight.

The midget submarines have failed to prove worthwhile. They had no impact on the battle and only hindered the plan. One was struck by Ward and another by Monaghan. Another was captured the next day, after Lieutenant Kazuo Sakamaki was observed to be spotted swimming ashore, thus being the very first American prisoner during that Second World War. Another was ejected following a traumatic injury sustained through a deep charge, and what happened to the fifth was not clear as of today.

America's humiliation

The attack's success was a humiliation to the Americans. The world's largest nation was unable to defend the strongest fortress in the world. The radar was not so well designed that it was not able to provide the advanced warnings it was capable of providing. In addition, the Harbour Intercept Centre was not connected to any decision-making system. The planes were stored in a manner that rendered rapid response impossible. Two of the key commanders refused to even think of a surprise attack as something that could be feasible.

In the end, the American response was exemplary. On the airfields as well as on the ships , the normal men as well as the junior officers were able to respond to the alert for air raids and general quarters call at a rapid pace. There were soldiers firing guns long before the warning about air raids. Some fired at the same time as the general quarters call. The average time for manning the guns was 5 minutes for battleships, 4 minutes to the cruisers, and 7 mins for destroyers.

A lot of ships were not operated and it was often up on junior officers to alarms that first rang. They repeatedly showed the courage, determination and decisiveness. The guns were in use until the very last moment. Control centres and engines were full until the water or fire finally drove the men out. Fighting fires was done with great risk to the personal. Men showed little care to their own safety when they pulled their fellow soldiers from flooded areas, casements or even the burning sea. If the Japanese were to have witnessed the courage and determination they displayed the day before, they could realize how foolish they were to wake up what is known as the sleeping giant.

The culprits

As scholar Gerhard Weinberg has pointed out that, If Oahu defeated his opponent Japanese strike, Short and Kimmel would have rushed to claim the glory. Therefore, they must take a lot of the responsibility for what transpired during Pearl Harbor. The job of Short was to guard the fleet. Kimmel was an identical, but larger job, but with a greater responsibility. Both were unsuccessful. Short was unable to conduct patrols that were at the highest level of his troops He also failed to incorporate the radar system within his command structure. the planes were kept on alert for four hours even though he was aware that he could not be sure to detect a possible attack until the attacker was only within an hour or less and he failed to create the system of designated areas to facilitate an arrival by American aircraft, making it difficult for his troops to differentiate friendly aircraft from non-friendly.

Kimmel was also unable to consider an attack from afar. He did not even take measures to secure his large vessels with anti-torpedo nets. Kimmel also was also a part of Short the failure to establish patrols. Kimmel operated the fleet like clockwork. Ships came and went following a predetermined pattern. He also allowed a schedule of 'surprise' alerts. Every single move of his fleet was predicted. Kimmel was astonished by the warnings Washington issued to him. Even though he was aware that there was a possibility of a Japanese assault on the Pacific was imminent , he did not detect anything sinister in possibility it was the Japanese were breaking the codes and changing significations and turning her fleet into silence on radios. There was nothing, it seemed, that would awaken him to enhance security in any way.

Washington was significantly better, but they fell short in two areas. They ought to have understood the urgent necessity of telling Kimmel regarding the Japanese concern about the positions of his vessels in the harbor. There will always be the choice in Washington not to call the scrambler phone and remind Oahu of the one-hour date that Nomura was to be given. Of course, Washington was concerned that the call would undermine Magic. In some ways Pearl Harbor was the cost of fighting Magic. (Churchill was faced with similar problems in his Ultra decrypts. Certain of them were not possible to act on without releasing what he described as the Crown Jewels'.)

There is a question of whether Roosevelt deliberately permitted the Japanese to strike Pearl Harbor in order to convince Congress to accept going to war. There's not enough space to disprove all the bizarre and ingenuous arguments used to justify this idea. Other than the fact that no one has presented any documentary evidence to support this theory this is a complete sham. The story goes that Roosevelt did not inform Kimmel and Short to induce the Japanese to strike. This is not true as If Roosevelt had wanted to join this war, he wouldn't be the first to arrange for the fleet of his destroyed. He would have advised Kimmel and Short to ensure that when the time for attack did occur, he could have won his war, but didn't lose his fleet. The truth is that no one in the highest authority could have predicted or even considered an attack that was plausible.

Chapter 9: Effects

America embraces war

When Americans discovered the news that Pearl Harbor had succumbed to an attack that was unexpected in shock, they were stunned by the news. A large portion of the initial anger was directed towards the government for misleading the American citizens. For many years, Americans were informed the idea that Pearl Harbor was an impregnable fortress. For a long time, they were believed that the navy was responsible for their safety. John Dingell, a Michigan representative, was a voice for many people when he called for the military court of navy and army commanders including Kimmel for the 'naval scandal'.

However, there was also a sense of satisfaction that tensions with Japan had been finally dissolved. After years of uncertainty and inaction America finally realized what it needed to do. Japan had cleared all doubts off.

In the case of the ships the damage was much less than what it appeared, due to two reasons.

First, six of eight battleships returned quickly back into service. (Arizona was too damaged to salvage and was relegated to the ruins. It is now an official memorial to war. Oklahoma was raised from its bottom , but it was never fixed.) In a way, Japan performed the Americans the favor of forcing them to rely more on their carriers during the following months following the war. The most famous combats of 1942 were intended to be battles between carriers. Midway only one year later showed America's dominance over the Pacific without or with battleships.

Furthermore, the Japanese attack unites an entire nation. Before the attack , there were many people in America who were unwaveringly opposed to fighting Japan. The most notable was Roosevelt was adamant to only declare war only if Japan made it a condition of America. However, it was the case that Pearl Harbor attack was so shocking and at an unprecedented scale that Roosevelt was no longer hesitant. On December 8, Roosevelt told Congress that the 7th of December, 1941 was a date that will be remembered forever'. He described the attack as 'unprovoked and insane' and requested Congress to declare war against Japan. The Congress obliged with the Senate having a vote of 82-0 in favor as well as it was the House of Representatives 388 to 1 in favor. Tokyo had handed down this vote in an manner that could not an American would have ever done.

Churchill is a friend of America

A just a few miles away was favorable to America's participation in the war. Churchill had been at Chequers eating dinner along with US Special Envoy Averell Harriman as well as US ambassador to London John Winant on the 7 December night. In the words of Harriman Churchill appeared exhausted and depressed'. He had a good reason for it to feel this way. While Britain can be proud of its "we stand by ourselves" attitude and look back with pride on its victory in the Battle of Britain of 1940 however, it was impossible that she could ever defeat Nazi Germany. In order to do so, Churchill required the full power of America.

When he turned to the radio to listen to the latest news , his ears were tingling at the mention of Japan and 'Hawaii' as well as an allusion to the Japanese fighting their fellow Americans'. He had waited for so long to get this news that his life was thrown into chaos and was close to calling war on Japan at the moment when Winant advised him that he required more than a radio broadcast as a reason. Within moments Churchill was calling to Roosevelt.

Japan has to face a'strategic as well as tactical catastrophe'

The American historian Gerhard Weinberg has called Japan's attack on Pearl Harbor 'a strategic and tactical failure'. Its rash and reckless attack within a matter of 24 hours devastated the entire might of America, Britain and the other allies against her. Pearl Harbor led directly to the Battle of the Coral Sea (7-8 May 1942) that severely damaged Japan's ability to carry out her next big project at Midway. In the Battle of Midway (4-7 June 1942), Japan suffered a major loss. Midway (4-7

June 1942) Japan suffered the loss of three ships. Japan believed that the American navy was weak and lacked in fighting spirit. But she was surprised to discover that she unleashed an unstoppable force strong commanders and brave seamen, backed by incredible industrial power of America.

Short and Kimmel endure the consequences.

Short and Kimmel Short Kimmel and Short, Kimmel the incident brought humiliation. They were freed from their duties on 16 December, and then pressured to request an early retirement. They accepted on February 22, 1942. Short passed away in 1949 in 1949, and Kimmel was killed in the year 1968. They were never charged with any wrongdoing, nor were they cleared of any wrongdoing. They were subject to the repeated efforts of a nation to determine who's fault the incident was. They were witnesses to or sat through eight inquiries over the course of time: The Roberts Commission (1941-2), The Hart Inquiry (1944), The Army Inquiry (1944), The Navy Inquiry (1944), The Clausen Investigation (1944-45),

The Hewitt Inquiry (1945), The Clarke Investigation (1944-45) and The Joint Congressional Committee Investigation (1945-46). In 1999, the Senate cleared Short and Kimmel by the vote of 52 votes to 47. The narrowness of the decision demonstrates the strength of the ongoing debate that continues to rage in America.

Pearl Harbor remains and will remain one of the most famous and dramatic naval battles in the history of warfare. It will continue to amaze us with the ugliness that was Pearl Harbor, for the brutality of Japanese strike, for the incompetence of local commanders, and for the bravery displayed by the personnel at the airfields, as well as in the vessels. When we revisit the battle , we are shocked by the speed at which the battle was conducted as well as the speed with which the massive battleships were destroyed and at the inexplicably absence of vigilance at the island. It was a crucial event in the Second World War. In less than two hours, the fate of a bloody conflict in Europe that was conceived by one of the greatest wicked men in the history of mankind, was tipping toward liberty and freedom. The declaration of war by the United States on Nazi Germany on 11 December 1941 was a sure sign it was a sign that days of Nazi oppression were over. This was how Pearl Harbor bring a ray of optimism to Europe during her darkest hours.

Chapter 10: What Happened To Take Place On The Day Of Pearl Harbor?

Pearl Harbor was the target of Pearl Harbor was an unanticipated military strike at the U.S.A. by the Imperial Japanese Navy Air Service on the US marine base in Pearl Harbor in Honolulu, in the Terrain of Hawaii, instantly before 08:00 on the Sunday of the seventh of December in 1941. It was a surprise attack for the U.S. was a neutral nation at the time however, the attack caused it into the war of World War II the following day. Through the planning process it was reported that the Japanese army's management described the attack in terms of Operation Z, the Hawaii Operation, Operation AI as well as Operation Z.

The attack was planned as a means of deterring the US Pacific Fleet from hindering Japan's planned army actions within Southeast Asia against the U.K. and the Netherlands and U.S.A. outside regions. Japan began joint attacks against the US-controlled Philippines, Guam, and Wake Island, and the British Empire in Malaya, Singapore, and Hong Kong, over the time of seven hours.

This complete guide will provide more information on the events that took place that triggered the Japanese as well as how United States reacted.

In the 7th hour, at 7:48 a.m. Hawaiian Time, the attack began (18:18 GMT). In two waves 353 Imperial Japanese airplanes (consisting of fighters level and dive bombers as well as torpedo bombers) taken from six carriers attack the central area. The entire fleet of 8 USA Navy battleships present were injured, with 4 one sinking. The other four, including that of the USS Arizona were later raised and six were recommissioned, and were used during the war. 3 destroyers, 3 cruisers as well as an anti-aircraft vessel for training and a minelayer also damaged or destroyed from the Japanese. In total, the 188 American aircrafts were destroyed 2400 people were killed and injuring

1,178 others. The dry dock, power plant and shipyard, as well as upkeep facilities storage for fuel and torpedo centers, and submarine piers as well as the head office building (which includes the security structure) were not the targets of the.

The Japanese experienced only small losses which included 29 aircrafts and five submarines that were midgets destroyed and 64 soldiers killed. One of the submarine's commanders, Kazuo Sakamaki, was captured.

On the same the next day (December 8 at Tokyo), Japan announced war against Japan, the USA in addition to the British Empire However, the declarations were not made public until the following day.

When they realized that their territory was also being attacked After seeing that their territory was also being attacked, the British federal government declared war on Japan as well as the US Congress declared the war against Japan on the same morning (December 8, 1918).).

Germany and Italy declared war against the USA on the 11th of December, regardless of the fact they had no legal obligation to declare war as part of the Tripartite Pact with Japan. In response, the U.S. responded by announcing the war against Germany as well as Italy.

There were numerous precedents for Japan's unexpected army action but the absence any warning from the government, especially as peace talks seemed to be advancing in the process, prompted the president Franklin D. Roosevelt to declare the 7th of December, 1941as "a day that is going to remain in infamy."

It was revealed that the attack at Pearl Harbor was ultimately announced as a war criminal act during the Tokyo Trials just because it occurred without a declaration of war or a warning.

The Beginning

In the 20th century, a dispute among Japan with in the U.S. had been a possibility both countries been anticipating and had prepared for. From the end of the 1890s onwards, Japan had been suspicious of American expansion of its army and territorial boundaries across areas like the Pacific and Asia which included the expansion of islands such that of Hawaii or the Philippines which they believed to be within or within their area of influence.

Even though Japan was beginning to hunt after a hostile attitude towards the US after the US' decision to reject the Racial Equality Proposition, the relationship between the two countries remained friendly enough to remain trading partners. The stress level didn't increase until Japan began to attack Manchuria in 1931. Japan moved into China in the following decade which led to the 2nd Sino-Japanese War in the year 1937. Japan took part in a joint effort to segregate China and gather independently-owned resources to win over the Chinese mainland. "Southern Operations "Southern Operation" was established to aid in these endeavors.

Things such as events like the Japanese attacks on USS Panay, the Allison incident and the Nanking Massacre moved Western popular opinion significantly against Japan from the beginning of November 1937. The U.S.A. planned a joint action along with the British to blockade Japan however it did not succeed. After the President Roosevelt's Franklin D. Roosevelt's request, American corporations stopped providing Japan with military equipment in 1938.

The Japanese attacked French Indochina in the year 1940, Japan tried to hamper the flow of merchandise to China. The USA prevented the export of parts, planes, equipment for devices, as well as air transportation gas Japan that Japan considered as an act of aggression.

But it was the U.S.A. was unable to block oil deliveries due to a widespread belief in Washington that such a decision could be seen as an extreme justification for the dependence of Japan on American oil.

The President Franklin D. Roosevelt moved the Pacific Fleet from San Diego to Hawaii in the middle of 1940s.

He also authorized an army build-up in the Philippines with the hope of preventing Japanese involvement in the area. Because that the Japanese high command considered (improperly) that a war against Singapore, the U.K.'s Southeast Asian people, particularly Singapore could bring in the U.S. into the war A lethal preemptive strike was seen as the only option to keep from American military involvement. Japanese war planners also considered that an invasion into the Philippines as a necessity. It was believed that the United States' War Plan Orange called for a 40,000-man elite force to defend the Philippines but this plan was never implemented due to objections by Douglas MacArthur, who really believed that he'd really require the strength of a 10x size.

By the year 1941, American organizers expected the Philippines would be a deserted country by the outbreak of war. Admiral Thomas C. Hart, director of the Asiatic Fleet, got orders to influence the Philippines later in that year.

After the taking in French Indochina after the fall of France The US ended up halting the export of oil to Japan in July 1941, largely because of the new American restrictions on the use of domestic oil.

Japan continued to work on plans to capture those oil rich Dutch East Indies because of this decision.

On the 17th of August Roosevelt advised Japan that in the event that "nearby nation" were attacked, America would react in the same way. The Japanese were given a choice to either withdraw from China and take the possibility of losing their face or seize fresh materials from Southeast Asia's rich resources European possessions.

Through the year 1941 Japan as well as the U.S.A. held talks to improve relations. After negotiating a deal in 1941 with Japan's Nationalist regime, Japan offered to withdraw from the countries of China as well as Indochina. It also suggested using its personal analysis of Tripartite Pact and avoiding trade discrimination in the event that all other countries were to follow the same guidelines. The idea was rejected in Roosevelt's White Home. The Japanese Premier Konoye later offered to meet with Roosevelt however Roosevelt declined because he wanted to make an agreement first. In the meantime, the U.S. envoy to Japan was able to push Roosevelt to agree to the meeting on a few occasions and claimed this was the sole method to keep the conciliation Konoye cabinet in place and to maintain Pacific peace. However, his suggestion was ignored. After it became clear that the

Japanese Army refused remove all troops from China The Konoye administration broke up in the next month.

The last proposal from Japan, made on November 20, proposed to have three countries, the U.S., UK, and Netherlands provide 1 million U.S.A. gallons (3.8 million liters) of fuel for air travel and increase their sanctions on Japan and cease aid from China with the intention of Japan pulling out of southern Indochina and to avoid threats on Southeast Asia. It was the Hull note, which was an American counter-proposal, dated 27 November (November 27th in Japan) demanded that Japan immediately withdraw from China as well as sign non-aggression agreements to Pacific states. The Japanese workforce left port to head for Pearl Harbor on November 26th which was the day before the note was issued.

The aim of the strike was to act to deter the USA Pacific Fleet from disrupting Japan's army-prepared efforts to strike in Southeast Asia against British, Dutch as well as United States foreign areas. Japan began joint attacks against the US-controlled Philippines, Guam, and Wake Island, and the British Empire in Malaya, Singapore, and Hong Kong, over the time of seven hours. Furthermore it was viewed an attack preemptive from Japan, Japanese, "before the oil gauge was shut off."

Admiral Isoroku Yamamoto, who was then the commander of the Japan's Combined Fleet, had started preliminary preparations in preparation for an invasion of Pearl Harbor to safeguard the advance through the "Southern Resource Area" (the Japanese classification of Southeast Asia, the Dutch East Indies and Southeast Asia generally) quite early in 1941.

Only after a long and arduous discussion with the Naval Head Office and a risk to leave his post, will General Staff of the Imperial Japanese Navy General Staff accept primary planning and training to prepare for attack.

In the spring of 1941, major planning was underway, led by the Back Admiral Rynosuke Kusaka with assistance by Lieutenant Minoru Genda and Yamamoto's Deputy Chief of Staff Capt. Kameto Kuroshima. They spent a significant amount of time researching the British air assault against the Italian fleet at Taranto in 1940.

Pilots were instructed, the devices were changed, and information was collected over the next couple of months. However, despite all these efforts however, Emperor Hirohito was able to defer the intrusion plan until November 5th, which was the 3rd of four Imperial Conferences that met to discuss about the matter. Following a large number of Japanese leaders warned to him that the "Hull Remember" could "ruin the fruit of the China event, jeopardize Manchukuo and weaken Japanese rule over Korea," the emperor granted his last approval on the 1st of December.

By the end of 1941, many people feared there was a war between US as well as Japan was imminent. Just prior to attacks on Pearl Harbor, a Gallup survey found fifty percent of Americans believed that war was imminent with Japan 27 percent did not however, as well as 21 percent who were unsure. Despite being aware the U.S. Pacific bases and roads were put in high alert numerous occasions, USA authorities questioned that Pearl Harbor would be the initial target. Instead the Philippines were believed to be first targeted. This assumption was based on the possibility that the air bases of the nation as well as the navy base in Manila are positioned for maritime passages as well as the delivery of goods to Japan from the south. They also believed, wrongly that Japan would not be able to undertake more than one major marine project at a given time.

The Japanese attack had a number of important objectives. In the first place, it intended to attack the most important American system of fleets, preventing it from stopping the Pacific Fleet from disrupting Japan's incursion into in the Dutch East Indies and Malaya and allowing Japan to take over Southeast Asia unrestricted. It was also intended to allow Japan to consolidate its position and strengthen its marine forces prior to it was 1940 when the Vinson-Walsh Act, which allowed shipbuilding and eliminated any chance of successful. Thirdly, battleships were picked as the main target to test America's ability to coordinate its forces across the Pacific because they were the most powerful ships in any navy of the time. In the end, it was thought that the attack would lower American spirit to the point that they would be less tolerant of Japan and the U.S.A. administration would desert its anti-Japanese stance and search to a peaceful resolution with Japan.

In the process of establishing at the Pacific Fleet at Pearl Harbor was not without its drawbacks. the ships that were targeted were in shallow waters and therefore relatively simple to repair and possibly fix as well as many of the sailors would be able to escape in the event that they were on leave or out of the port. Another major drawback was the absence from Pearl Harbor of all 3 carriers in the U.S.A. Pacific Fleet (Business, Lexington, and Saratoga). Admiral Mahan's "definitive fight" doctrine, with the specific goal of destroying the most effective number of battleships accepted by the IJN's top brass. Despite these reservations, Yamamoto chose to go forward with the plan.

Other port targets such as but not limited to the naval garden, the oil tank farms, and the submarine station, were largely ignored because they thought that the war was finished before the impact of these setups could be observed.

The Attack

In the 20th century, a dispute in the 1920s between Japan as well as Japan and the U.S. had been a possibility both nations anticipated and planned for. From the end of the 1890s onwards, Japan had been suspicious of American military and territorial expansion throughout Asia and the Pacific and Asia which included the addition of islands such as Hawaii as well as the Philippines they believed to be within their area of influence.

Despite being aware that Japan was beginning to go after a hostile posture towards the U.S.A. after the denial by the Racial Equality Proposition, the two nations' relations remained friendly enough to remain trading with each other. There was no significant increase in tension until Japan began to attack Manchuria in 1931. Japan expanded into China over the next decade which led to the 2nd Sino-Japanese War in the year 1937. Japan took part in a joint effort to divide China and gather sufficient resources for independent an outcome on mainland. "Southern Operation "Southern Operation" was created to aid in these endeavors.

The events like the Japanese assault on USS Panay, the Allison incident, and the Nanking Massacre moved Western popular opinion significantly against Japan from the beginning of the December month in 1937. The U.S.A. was preparing a joint action along with the British to blockade Japan however it failed. In response to the president Roosevelt's Franklin D. Roosevelt's request, American corporations stopped providing Japan with army equipment in 1938.

Involved in French Indochina in the year 1940, Japan tried to hamper the flow of merchandise to China. The U.S.A. prohibited exports of elements, aircrafts as well as device tools as well as air travel fuel to Japan in what Japan considered to be a hostile act.

However the U.S.A. did not stop the oil supply due to the widespread belief within Washington that such an act could be considered an extreme justification for the dependence of Japan on American oil.

Former President Franklin D. Roosevelt transferred the Pacific Fleet from San Diego to Hawaii in the middle of 1940s.

He also authorized an army to accumulate in the Philippines and the Philippines, all in the hope of stopping Japanese incursions into the area. Simply because Japan's Japanese high command believed (improperly) that a war against the British Southeast Asian groups, specifically Singapore and Singapore, could bring the USA into war, a fatal preventive strike seemed to be the only option to keep out American military involvement. Japanese war planners also considered an intrusion into the Philippines to be necessary. It was believed that the United States' War Plan Orange called for a 40,000-man elite force to defend the Philippines but this plan was never executed because of the objections of Douglas MacArthur, who actually believed that he really needed an army 10 times the size.

By the year 1941, American organizers expected the Philippines to be abandoned by the beginning of the war. Admiral Thomas C. Hart, commander of the Asiatic Fleet, got orders to make an impact later in the year.

After the capture of French Indochina after the fall of France Following the fall of France, the U.S. ultimately stopped exporting oil to Japan during the month of July 1941, partly because of the recent American restrictions on the consumption of oil in the U.S.

Japan continued to prepare to take over those oil rich Dutch East Indies due to this decision.

On the 17th of August Roosevelt informed Japan that in the event that "nearby countries" were attacked, America would react in similar fashion. The Japanese were given a choice of withdrawing from China and take the risk of losing its face or take fresh, basic items from Southeast Asia's rich in resources European possessions.

At the time of the war in 1941, Japan and the U.S. were in discussions to strengthen relations.

After they reached an agreement in the course of negotiations with an agreement with the Nationalist Administration, Japan offered to withdraw from the majority of China in the region and Indochina. It also recommended making its own assessment of the Tripartite Pact and avoiding trade discrimination if other countries were to follow the same. These suggestions were rejected from Roosevelt's White Home. The Japanese Premier Konoye later offered to discuss the matter with Roosevelt however Roosevelt did not accept the offer because he was looking to negotiate a deal first. Roosevelt's U.S. envoy to Japan was able to convince Roosevelt to agree to the conference at times in the belief the conference was the best method to keep the conciliation Konoye cabinet at the helm and to maintain Pacific peace. However, his suggestion was ignored. After it became clear that the Japanese military refused remove all troops from China and China, the Konoye administration broke up in the next month.

The final proposal of Japan's, which was made on the 20th of November, suggested for it be requested that the U.S., UK, and Netherlands supply 1 million USA gallons (3.8 million liters) of fuel for air travel and increase their sanctions on Japan and cease aid from China as a condition to Japan pulling out of southern Indochina and to avoid attack within Southeast Asia. It was the Hull note, which was an American counter-proposal, dated 27 November (November 27th in Japan) demanded that Japan immediately withdraw from China as well as sign non-aggression agreements to Pacific states. The Japanese workforce left port to head for Pearl Harbor on November 26th on the day prior to the date the note was released.

The aim of the strike was to act to deter the USA Pacific Fleet from hindering Japan's military preparations within Southeast Asia against British, Dutch as well as U.S. foreign areas. Japan began joint attacks against the U.S.-controlled Philippines, Guam, and Wake Island,

and also the British Empire in Malaya, Singapore, and Hong Kong, over the duration of 7 hours. Furthermore, it was thought to be as a preemptive strike by Japanese, "before the oil gauge was shut off."

Admiral Isoroku Yamamoto, at the time commanding the Japan's Combined Fleet, had started preliminary preparations to launch an assault on Pearl Harbor to safeguard the advance to the "Southern Resource Area" (the Japanese classification of that area, which includes the Dutch East Indies and Southeast Asia generally) quite early in 1941.

After a lengthy wrangling with the Naval Head Office and a threat to lose his command will General Staff of the Imperial Japanese Navy General Staff accept primary planning and training in preparation for an offensive.

In the spring of 1941, the full-scale preparations began, spearheaded by the Back Admiral

Rynosuke Kusaka, assisted by Captain Minoru Genda, Yamamoto's Deputy Chief of Staff Lieutenant Kameto Kuroshima. Strategic planners spent great deal of time looking at the British air strike against the Italian fleet at Taranto during the year 1940.

Pilots were instructed, technology were changed, and information was collected over the next couple of months. However, despite all these efforts however, Emperor Hirohito was able to defer the intrusion plan until November 5th, which was the third of the four Imperial Conferences that met to discuss over the issue. Following a large number of Japanese leaders warned to him that the "Hull Remember" plan could "damage the results of the China incident and put at risk Manchukuo and weaken Japanese control over Korea," the emperor approved the plan on the 1st of December.

At the end of 1941, many observers were concerned an imminent war between USA as well as Japan was coming up. Prior to attacks on Pearl Harbor, a Gallup survey revealed the fact that 53 percent of Americans were expecting war with Japan 27 percent did not but 21 percent were uncertain. In spite of being aware the U.S. Pacific bases and road networks had been placed on alert many occasions, USA authorities questioned that Pearl Harbor would be the first target. Instead it was believed that the Philippines were believed to be first targeted. The reason for this was the risk that the air bases as well as the navy base in Manila could pose to sea-going vessels and materials to Japan from the south. They also assumed, wrongly they believed that Japan was unable to carry out more than one important marine project at the same time.

It was clear that the Japanese attack had a number of important objectives. It was aimed to harm the vital American naval systems by thus preventing from preventing the Pacific Fleet from disrupting Japan's incursion into Malaya and the Dutch East Indies and Malaya and allowing Japan to conquer Southeast Asia unrestricted. In addition, it was supposed to give time to Japan to join forces and strengthen its marine force before it was 1940 when the Vinson-Walsh Act, which allowed shipbuilding to cease, eliminating any chance of successful. Thirdly, battleships were chosen as the main targets for a strike against America's capacity to coordinate its forces across the Pacific due to them being the top ships of any navy of the time. In the end, it was believed that the strike could weaken American morale enough so that USA administration would abandon its anti-Japanese stance and search to a peaceful solution with Japan.

The decision to strike with the Pacific Fleet at Pearl Harbor was not without its drawbacks. The ships targeted were located in shallow water which made them relatively simple to repair and possibly fix. Additionally, many of sailors would abandon the area because they were on leave from the coast or being rescued from the haven. Another significant disadvantage was the absence of Pearl Harbor of all 3 warships of the USA Pacific Fleet

(Business, Lexington Saratoga, and Business Saratoga). Admiral Mahan's "definitive battle" doctrine, particularly his goal of degrading the most battleships, was accepted by the IJN's top brass. Despite these reservations, Yamamoto chose to go forward with the plan.

Other port targets that included the naval garden and oil tank farms and the submarine station, were ignored because they believed that the war was finished before the effects of these setups could be observed.

The effects of the attack afterward

Captain Homer N. Wallin was assigned to lead an official salvage mission following an extensive search for survivors.

Divers working for The Navy (coast as well as tenders) and at the Pearl Harbor Naval Shipyard, and civilian experts (Pacific Bridge Company, and others) started working on ships that were able to be brought back to floating in the vicinity of Pearl Harbor. They repaired holes, cleaned up debris, and then drained the out the water from ships. Divers from the Navy performed work inside the damaged vessels. 5 battleships as well as 2 cruisers got covered and refloated in six months, allowing them to be transported into shipyards located in Pearl Harbor and the mainland to undergo a thorough repair.

The extensive healing process lasted for another year, resulting in around 20,000 man hours submerged.

Arizona and the ship that was targeted Utah were severely damaged to be repaired, so they were both sunk in the year 1947, with Arizona acting as a war memorial. Although Oklahoma was raised in a timely manner however, it never repaired and sank in 1947, while being towed towards the mainland. Nevada was Nevada was extremely difficult to raise or fix and 2 members of the team passed away from breathing in harmful vapors that had accumulated within the vessel's interior. In the event that it was it was possible, devices and weapons were recovered from damaged vessels and used in other vessels.

2.22 p.m. Eastern time (8:52 a.m. Hawaiian time), White Home Press Secretary Stephen Early made the following announcement: "The Japanese have assaulted Pearl Harbor from the air as well as all military and marine activities on the island of Oahu which is the principal American base on the Hawaiian islands."

Through this afternoon Early gave additional announcements to the approximately 150 White Home press reporters when information became available.

Around 2.25 p.m. Eastern time, first reports of the attack began to circulate across news wires. Around 22:30 p.m. Eastern time, the CBS radio network's scheduled show, World News Today, broadcast the first radio report (which was, in the moment, offered the most earliest alternative for ordinary people to find out more about the incident). The report was broadcast was read in the voice of John Charles Daly, who later returned to London for a discussion, in which Robert Trout improvised on the anticipated London response. In the 2nd quarter of 2.33 p.m. Eastern time, the initial report of NBC changed into an opera, a dramatic from The Inspector-General, and lasted just 21 seconds. There were no abrupt interruptions of industrially-planned programming contrary to the later regular with significant developments in the news.

An account on paper that coexists with the original one linked the incident with that of the Battle of Port Arthur, 37 years prior, when an Imperial Japanese Navy assaulted the Imperial Russian Navy and triggered to start the Russo-Japanese War.

Modern writers have gone on to draw distinctions between attacks, but with greater neutrality.

Roosevelt delivered his famous Day of Infamy speech to an Joint Session of Congress the day following the attack, which demanded an official declaration of war against Japan. Japanese Empire. In less than an hour, Congress gave his demand. Even though it was not required by the Tripartite Pact didn't demand it, Germany and Italy announced war against U.S.A. U.S.A. on December 11.

On the same the same day Congress issued a declaration of war on Germany as well as Italy.

The U.K. had been at war with Germany from September 1939, and also with Italy since June 1940 as well. British Premier Winston Churchill had threatened to declare war against Germany and the USA "within the time" in the event of an Japanese attack.

When Churchill was informed of his knowledge of Japanese attack against Malaya, Singapore, and Hong Kong, he chose that there was no reason to wait or consult authorities in the U.S.A. administration any longer and immediately contacted the Japanese Ambassador right away. In the aftermath, the UK declared the war against Japan nine hours before that of the United States.

The entire Allies from the Pacific Theater were shocked by the initial strike. The frightful situation was exacerbated by the loss of more troops. A few hours later, Japan began an attack on in the Philippines (because due to the time difference that it was the 8th of December on The Philippines). It was the battleships Prince of Wales and Repulse were destroyed in the waters of Malaya within three days of an attack at Pearl Harbor, prompting Churchill to declare later "I have never had more direct shock than at the time of war. The full remorse of the news shook me when I sat up and turned in my the bed. Except for people like the

American victims of Pearl Harbor who were hurrying back to California and back, there were neither British nor American capital vessels within Pacific or Indian Ocean. Indian Ocean or Pacific. Japan was the supreme power over this huge stretch of water, and we were all naive and defenseless."

Pearl Harbor was commonly referenced in American propaganda throughout the war.

Another result that resulted from the assault at Pearl Harbor and its consequences (specifically the Niihau incident) was the removal of Japanese-Americans and their families into the adjacent internment camps. Many Japanese-American leaders were detained and sent to camps with high security, which included Sand Island at the mouth of the Honolulu port, and Kilauea Armed force Camp on the island of Hawaii within days of the attack.

There were more than 110,000 Japanese Americans, essentially all of them living in the

West Coast, were ultimately arrested, however only 1,200 to 1,800 were held in Hawaii even though Japanese Americans made up more than one third of the population.

The incident had global consequences as well. There was a global impact as well. Pacific Ocean bordering Canadian province British Columbia has long had significant numbers of Japanese immigrants as well as their descendants from Japan-Canadians. It was during the time of Pearl Harbor attack increased pre-war tensions, prompting a response by government officials from the Canadian Federal government. In the War Steps Act, Order-in-Council P.C. no. 1486 was published on February 24, 1942. It allowed the mandatory removal of all Canadians with Japanese origin of Japanese heritage from British Columbia, and stopping their return. On March 4 the requirements of the Act for the deportation of Japanese-Canadians were enacted. In the end, around 12,000 people were moved into camps for the interior and 2,000 were sent to road camps, and a further

22,000 were forced to work on sugar beet fields in the plains.

The American soldiers who distinguished themselves during the battle in the battle of Pearl Harbor were rewarded fifteen Medals of Honor, 51 Navy Crosses and 53 Silver Stars, 4 Navy and Marine Corps Medals One Differentiated Flying Star, four Distinguished Service Awards, one Distinguished Service Medal, and 3 Bronze Star Medals within the aftermath from the assault.

A Pearl Harbor Celebration Medal which was a distinctive military award, was given to all soldiers who were veterans of the attack.

The Japanese organizing team for Pearl Harbor's Pearl Harbor attack determined that there was a way to save pilots whose aircrafts had been too severely damaged in order to get back to their service rescuers was needed. The island of Niihau was selected as the location for rescue because it was just a half hour's travel time away far from Pearl Harbor.

In the incident on Wheeler Lieutenant Shigenori Nishikaichi of Hiryu's 0 was wounded, so his plane flew him to the site of rescue. The aircraft suffered a lot of damage when it arrived. A member of the region Hawaiians was able to save Nishikaichi out of the rubble and retrieved the weapon of the pilot maps, codes, and other documents, recognizing they were aware that both they knew that the U.S. and Japan were in danger. The inhabitants of the island were not able to access phones or radios, and therefore were unaware about attacks on Pearl Harbor. To obtain the files, Nishikaichi sought the assistance of three Japanese-Americans. Nishikaichi was killed, while an Hawaiian civilian was injured in the fights that took place One of the three partners took his own life, while his companion and the third member were incarcerated.

www.ingramcontent.com/pod-product-compliance
Lightning Source LLC
Chambersburg PA
CBHW050023130526
44590CB00042B/1871